THE DECLARATION OF ARBROATH

M CCC XX

THE
DECLARATION
OF
ARBROATH

SIR JAMES FERGUSSON, Bart

formerly Keeper of the Records of Scotland

EDINBURGH

AT THE UNIVER-

SITY PRESS

CONTENTS

v

LIST OF ILLUSTRATIONS

The endpapers show part of the draft text of the Declaration, from the Brechin Castle *Scotichronicon*.

INTRODUCTION

THERE IS NO SCOTTISH historical document, unless it be the National Covenant of 1638, whose name at least is better known to the average Scotsman than the Declaration of Arbroath. Such is the popular name of the Letter of the barons of Scotland to Pope John XXII dated at Arbroath on 6 April 1320. One of its main sentences, 'Never will we on any conditions be brought under English rule', is, in one form or another, often quoted out of context as a modern defiance, if the speaker is inclined to equate the Parliament of Great Britain, because it sits in the distant south of England, with 'English rule'. Another sentence, in praise of freedom, is inscribed in large letters on the war memorial of the Royal Scots in Edinburgh.

Thus many know of the Letter who have never read through a translation of it. Few realize that it was framed as a letter, not as a basic constitutional document, to meet a political and diplomatic crisis during a pause in the long War of Independence which Scotland waged from 1297 to 1328. But however ignorant of its significance they are right to revere it. It is its call upon eternal principles to meet the emergency of an occasion that has made it immortal, like Nelson's signal before Trafalgar or Lincoln's words over the graves at Gettysburg.

Not all who quote the Declaration of Arbroath have even seen the actual surviving document of its text, though it has been on public exhibition in the heart of Edinburgh for well over a century. But virtually every educated person in Scotland knows at least the fact of its existence and its essential terms—a declaration of unwavering support for King Robert Bruce and of resolution to maintain the independence of Scotland. Outside Scotland it is probably little heard of; but in Scotland it is regarded with the same veneration, the same belief in its fundamental character as a constitutional document, and the same incomplete understanding of its nature, as Magna Carta in England.

Historians who have studied the Letter have for nearly three hundred years been united in their admiration of it. It is recognized as a masterpiece of propaganda, of diplomacy, and more recently of mediaeval Latin prose. I am not now concerned to write of the first two of these aspects of it nor of its place, though it is an

I

INTRODUCTION

important one, in the development in European history of the concept of nationalism. I propose to examine the text. For to establish a text as accurately as possible is the essential preliminary to discussion of its contents.

I begin therefore by giving the Latin in full, in a form which, as I shall explain later, I believe to be the nearest possible reconstruction of the final version of the Letter, no longer extant, that actually went to Pope John XXII at Avignon, faced by a translation into modern English. Next I shall explain the background to the Letter and the circumstances in which it was drawn up, after which I shall offer the new information concerning them which I believe can be deduced from a study of the text in greater depth than has till now been possible. I shall give examples of significant variations in the text, and then an account of how the hitherto accepted text has been treated by its editors.

Readers who have no Latin will not, I hope, find these chapters too hard to follow. But since they are founded on an attempt to correct the Latin text of the Declaration of Arbroath, that attempt must be submitted to the judgment of better mediaeval scholars and better Latinists that I can claim to be. For them a variorum text is placed at the end of the book, showing exactly how I have amended the text and from what sources.

I wish to acknowledge the valuable help I have had from Professor Geoffrey Barrow, who holds the Chair of Mediaeval History in the University of Newcastle-upon-Tyne and who kindly read and commented on an early draft of this book. It owes much to his great work *Robert Bruce and the Community of the Realm of Scotland* (1965), which has so profoundly explored and enlightened the history of the Scottish War of Independence; but its opinion and speculations are, of course, my own. I also record my great indebtedness to Mr John Imrie, Keeper of the Records of Scotland, for many valuable suggestions and for much kind help in the final revision; and my thanks to Her Majesty's Stationery Office for permission to reproduce my English version of the Declaration and the photograph of the Register House document, both already published for the Scottish Record Office. I also acknowledge the kind permission of the Earl of Dalhousie to reproduce part of the *Scotichronicon* MS belonging to him and now preserved in the Register House.

I

THE DECLARATION OF ARBROATH.

LATIN TEXT RECONSTRUCTED.

ENGLISH TRANSLATION.

THE FRAMING OF THE

DECLARATION.

Capitals and spelling are as in the only surviving contemporary copy. The division into paragraphs is my own, as is the punctuation. Readers accustomed to classical Latin will note that mediaeval writers were a little unorthodox in their spelling. Here they will find e for ae, often c in place of t, and sometimes i and j or u and v interchanged.

Names marked with an asterisk are those for which on the Register House copy the seals still survive. David, Lord of Brechin, having perhaps mislaid his own seal, used that of Mary Ramsay, his second wife.

SANCTISSIMO PATRI IN CHRISTO AC DOMINO, DOMINO Johanni, diuina prouidencia Sacrosauncte Romane et Vniuersalis Ecclesie Summo Pontifici, Filii Sui Humiles et deuoti Duncanus Comes de Fyf, Thomas Ranulphi Comes Morauie, Dominus Mannie et Vallis Anandie, Patricius de Dumbar Comes Marchie★, Malisius Comes de Stratheryne★, Malcolmus Comes de Leuenax★, Willelmus Comes de Ross, Magnus Comes Cathanie et Orkadie et Willelmus Comes Suthirlandie; Walterus Senescallus Scocie, Willelmus de Soules Buttelarius Scocie, Jacobus Dominus de Duglas, Rogerus de Moubray★, Dauid Dominus de Brechyn★, Dauid de Graham★, Ingeramus de Vmfrauille★, Johannes de Menetethe Custos Comitatus de Menetethe, Alexander Fraser★, Gilbertus de Haya Constabularius Scocie★, Robertus de Keth Marescallus Scocie, Henricus de Sancto Claro, Johannes de Graham, Dauid de Lindesay, Willelmus Olifaunt★, Patricius de Graham★, Johannes de Fentoun, Willelmus de Abirnithy, Dauid de Wemys, Willelmus de Montefixo, Fergusius de Ardrossane, Eustachius de Maxwell, Willelmus de Ramesay, Willelmus de Montealto, Alanus de Morauia, Douenaldus Cambell, Johannes Cambrun, Reginaldus le chen★, Alexander de Setoun★, Andreas de Lescelyne et Alexander de Stratoun, Ceterique Barones et Liberetenentes ac tota Communitas Regni Scocie, omnimodam Reuerenciam filialem cum deuotis Pedum osculis beatorum.

My translation is not absolutely word for word nor phrase for phrase. One of the Declaration's marvels is the amount that it manages to say, even with the economy of expression that Latin permits, in only thirty-three lines (admittedly long ones). The Latin is a remarkably closely knitted texture, in very long sentences with many involved internal clauses. I have accordingly broken it down into paragraphs and some of its long sentences into shorter ones, trying, like previous translators, to bring out the emphasis on special points which the original so skilfully conveys. Both the range and the subtlety of the Letter can be to some extent indicated; but the sonorous music of its Latin, the sweep and cadence of the original sentences, are scarcely possible to reproduce. Yet it was, after all, meant to be read aloud, its language pleads to be declaimed, and any translator must bear this in mind.

To The Most Holy Father and Lord in Christ, the Lord John, by divine providence Supreme Pontiff of the Holy Roman and Universal Church, his humble and devout sons Duncan, Earl of Fife, Thomas Randolph, Earl of Moray, Lord of Man and of Annandale, Patrick Dunbar, Earl of March★, Malise, Earl of Strathearn★, Malcolm, Earl of Lennox★, William, Earl of Ross, Magnus, Earl of Caithness and Orkney, and William, Earl of Sutherland; Walter, Steward of Scotland, William Soules, Butler of Scotland, James, Lord of Douglas, Roger Mowbray★, David, Lord of Brechin★, David Graham★, Ingram Umfraville★, John Menteith, guardian of the earldom of Menteith, Alexander Fraser★, Gilbert Hay, Constable of Scotland★, Robert Keith, Marischal of Scotland, Henry St Clair, John Graham, David Lindsay, William Oliphant★, Patrick Graham★, John Fenton, William Abernethy, David Wemyss, William Mushet, Fergus of Ardrossan, Eustace Maxwell, William Ramsay, William Mowat, Alan Murray, Donald Campbell, John Cameron, Reginald Cheyne★, Alexander Seton★, Andrew Leslie, and Alexander Straiton, and the other barons and freeholders and the whole community of the realm of Scotland send all manner of filial reverence, with devout kisses of his blessed feet.

Scimus, Sanctissime Pater et Domine, et ex antiquorum gestis
et libris Colligimus quod inter Ceteras naciones egregias nostra
scilicet Scottorum nacio multis preconijs fuerit insignita, que de
Maiori Schithia per Mare tirenum et Columpnas Herculis trans-
iens et in Hispania inter ferocissimas gentes per multa temporum
curricula Residens a nullis quantumcumque barbaricis poterat
allicubi gentibus subiugari. Indeque veniens post mille et ducentos
annos a transitu populi israelitici per mare rubrum sibi sedes in
Occidente quas nunc optinet, expulsis primo Britonibus et Pictis
omnino deletis, licet per Norwagienses, Dacos et Anglicos sepius
inpugnata fuerit, multis cum victorijs et Laboribus quamplurimis
adquisiuit, ipsasque ab omni seruitute liberas, vt Priscorum
testantur Historie, semper tenuit. In quorum Regno Centum et
Tresdecim Reges de ipsorum Regali prosapia, nullo alienigena
interueniente, Regnauerunt.

Quorum Nobilitates et Merita, licet ex aliis non clarerent,
satis patenter effulgent ex eo quod Rex Regum et dominancium
dominus Jhesus Christus post passionem suam et Resurreccionem
ipsos in vltimis terre finibus constitutos quasi primos ad suam
fidem sanctissimam conuocauit. Nec eos per quemlibet in dicta
fide confirmari voluit set per suum primum apostolum vocacione
quamuis ordine secundum vel tercium, sanctum Andream
mitissimum beati Petri Germanum, quem semper ipsis preesse
voluit vt Patronum.

Hec autem Sanctissimi Patres et Predecessores vestri sollicita
mente pensantes ipsum Regnum et populum vt beati Petri germani peculium multis fauoribus et priuilegijs quamplurimis
Munierunt, Ita quippe quod gens nostra sub ipsorum proteccione
hactenus libera deguit et quieta donec ille Princeps Magnificus
Rex Anglorum Edwardus, pater istius qui nunc est, Regnum
nostrum acephalum populumque nullius mali aut doli conscium
nec bellis aut insultibus tunc assuetum sub amici et confederati
specie inimicabiliter infestauit. Cuius iniurias, Cedes, violencias,
predaciones, incendia, prelatorum incarceraciones, Monasteriorum
combustiones, Religiosorum spoliaciones et occisiones alia quoque
enormia et innumera que in dicto populo exercuit, nulli parcens

Most Holy Father and Lord, we know and from the chronicles and books of the ancients we find that among other famous nations our own, the Scots, has been graced with widespread renown. They journeyed from Greater Scythia by way of the Tyrrhenian Sea and the Pillars of Hercules, and dwelt for a long course of time in Spain among the most savage tribes, but nowhere could they be subdued by any race, however barbarous. Thence they came, twelve hundred years after the people of Israel crossed the Red Sea, to their home in the west where they still live today. The Britons they first drove out, the Picts they utterly destroyed, and, even though very often assailed by the Norwegians, the Danes and the English, they took possession of that home with many victories and untold efforts; and, as the historians of old time bear witness, they have held it free of all bondage ever since. In their kingdom there have reigned one hundred and thirteen kings of their own royal stock, the line unbroken by a single foreigner.

The high qualities and deserts of these people, were they not otherwise manifest, gain glory enough from this: that the King of kings and Lord of lords, our Lord Jesus Christ, after His Passion and Resurrection, called them, even though settled in the uttermost parts of the earth, almost the first to His most holy faith. Nor would He have them confirmed in that faith by merely anyone but by the first of His Apostles — by calling, though second or third in rank — the most gentle Saint Andrew, the Blessed Peter's brother, and desired him to keep them under his protection as their patron for ever.

The Most Holy Fathers your predecessors gave careful heed to these things and bestowed many favours and numerous privileges on this same kingdom and people, as being the special charge of the Blessed Peter's brother. Thus our nation under their protection did indeed live in freedom and peace up to the time when that mighty prince the King of the English, Edward, the father of the one who reigns today, when our kingdom had no head and our people harboured no malice or treachery and were then unused to wars or invasions, came in the guise of a friend and ally to harass them as an enemy. The deeds of cruelty, massacre, violence, pillage, arson, imprisoning prelates, burning down monasteries, robbing and killing monks and nuns, and yet other outrages without number

7

etati aut sexui, Religioni aut ordini, nullus scriberet nec ad
plenum intelligeret nisi quem experiencia informaret.

A quibus Malis innumeris, ipso Juuante qui post uulnera
medetur et sanat, liberati sumus per strenuissimum Principem,
Regem et Dominum nostrum, Dominum Robertum, qui pro
populo et hereditate suis de manibus Inimicorum liberandis quasi
alter Machabeus aut Josue labores et tedia, inedias et pericula,
leto sustinuit animo. Quem eciam diuina disposicio et iuxta leges
et Consuetudines nostras, quas vsque ad mortem sustinere
volumus, Juris successio et debitus nostrorum omnium Consensus
et Assensus nostrum fecerunt Principem atque Regem, cui tanquam illi per quem salus in populo nostro facta est pro nostra
libertate tuenda tam Jure quam meritis tenemur et volumus in
omnibus adherere.

Quem si ab inceptis desisteret, Regi Anglorum aut Anglicis nos
aut Regnum nostrum volens subicere, tanquam Inimicum nostrum et sui nostrique Juris subuersorem statim expellere niteremur et alium Regem nostrum qui ad defensionem nostram
sufficeret faceremus. Quia quamdiu Centum ex nobis viui remanserint, nuncquam Anglorum dominio aliquatenus volumus
subiugari. Non enim propter gloriam, diuicias aut honores pugnamus set propter libertatem solummodo quam Nemo bonus nisi
simul cum vita amittit.

Hinc est, Reuerende Pater et Domine, quod sanctitatem
vestram omni precum instancia genuflexis cordibus exoramus
quatinus sincero corde Menteque pia recensentes quod apud eum
cuius vices in terris geritis cum non sit Pondus nec distinccio
Judei et greci, Scoti aut Anglici, tribulaciones et angustias nobis
et Ecclesie dei illatas ab Anglicis paternis occulis intuentes,
Regem Anglorum, cui sufficere debet quod possidet cum olim
Anglia septem aut pluribus solebat sufficere Regibus, Monere et
exhortari dignemini vt nos scotos, in exili degentes Scocia vltra
quam habitacio non est nichilque nisi nostrum Cupientes, in
pace dimittat. Cui pro nostra procuranda quiete quicquid possumus, ad statum nostrum Respectu habito, facere volumus
cum effectu.

which he committed against our people, sparing neither age nor sex, religion nor rank, no one could describe nor fully imagine unless he had seen them with his own eyes.

But from these countless evils we have been set free, by the help of Him Who though He afflicts yet heals and restores, by our most tireless Prince, King and Lord, the Lord Robert. He, that his people and his heritage might be delivered out of the hands of our enemies, met toil and fatigue, hunger and peril, like another Maccabaeus or Joshua and bore them cheerfully. Him, too, divine providence, his right of succession according to our laws and customs which we shall maintain to the death, and the due consent and assent of us all have made our Prince and King. To him, as to the man by whom salvation has been wrought unto our people, we are bound both by law and by his merits that our freedom may be still maintained, and by him, come what way, we mean to stand.

Yet if he should give up what he has begun, and agree to make us or our kingdom subject to the King of England or the English, we should exert ourselves at once to drive him out as our enemy and a subverter of his own rights and ours, and make some other man who was well able to defend us our King; for, as long as but a hundred of us remain alive, never will we on any conditions be brought under English rule. It is in truth not for glory, nor riches, nor honours that we are fighting, but for freedom—for that alone, which no honest man gives up but with life itself.

Therefore it is, Reverend Father and Lord, that we beseech your Holiness with our most earnest prayers and suppliant hearts, inasmuch as you will in your sincerity and goodness consider all this, that, since with Him Whose vice-gerent on earth you are there is neither weighing nor distinction of Jew and Greek, Scotsman or Englishman, you will look with the eyes of a father on the troubles and privations brought by the English upon us and upon the Church of God. May it please you to admonish and exhort the King of the English, who ought to be satisfied with what belongs to him since England used once to be enough for seven kings or more, to leave us Scots in peace, who live in this poor little Scotland, beyond which there is no dwelling-place at all, and covet nothing but our own. We are sincerely willing to do anything for him, having regard to our condition, that we can, to win peace for ourselves.

Vestra enim interest, sancte Pater, hoc facere qui paganorum
feritatem, Christianorum culpis exigentibus, in Christianos
seuientem aspicitis et Christianorum terminos arctari indies,
quantumque vestre sanctitatis memorie derogat si (quod absit)
Ecclesia in aliqua sui parte vestris temporibus patiatur eclipsim
aut Scandalum, vos videritis. Excitet igitur Christianos Principes
qui non causam vt causam ponentes se fingunt in subsidium terre
sancte propter guerras quas habent cum proximis ire non posse.
Cuius inpedimenti Causa est verior quod in Minoribus proximis
debellandis vtilitas propior et resistencia debilior estimantur.
Set quam leto corde dictus dominus Rex noster et Nos si Rex
Anglorum nos in pace dimitteret illuc iremus qui nichil ignorat
satis novit. Quod Christi vicario totique Christianitati ostendimus et testamur.

Quibus si sanctitas vestra Anglorum relatibus nimis credula
fidem sinceram non adhibeat aut ipsis in nostram confusionem
fauere non desinat, corporum excidia, animarum exicia, et cetera
que sequentur incomoda que ipsi in nobis et Nos in ipsis fecerimus
vobis ab altissimo credimus inputanda.

Ex quo sumus et erimus in hiis que tenemur tanquam obediencie filii vobis tanquam ipsius vicario parati in omnibus complacere, ipsique tanquam Summo Regi et Judici causam nostram
tuendam committimus, Cogitatum nostrum Jactantes in ipso
sperantesque firmiter quod in nobis virtutem faciet et ad nichilum
rediget hostes nostros.

Sanctitatem ac sanitatem vestram conseruet altissimus
Ecclesie sue sancte per tempora diuturna.

Datum apud Monasterium de Abirbrothoc in Scocia sexto die
mensis Aprilis Anno gracie Millesimo Trescentesimo vicesimo
Anno vero Regni Regis nostri supradicti Quinto decimo.

This truly concerns you, Holy Father, since you see the savagery of the heathen raging against the Christians, as the sins of Christians have indeed deserved, and the frontiers of Christendom being pressed inward every day; and how much it will tarnish your Holiness's memory if (which God forbid) the Church suffers eclipse or scandal in any branch of it during your time, you must perceive. Then rouse the Christian princes who for false reasons pretend that they cannot go to the help of the Holy Land because of wars they have on hand with their neighbours. The real reason that prevents them is that in making war on their smaller neighbours they find quicker profit and weaker resistance. But how cheerfully our Lord the King and we too would go there if the King of the English would leave us in peace, He from Whom nothing is hidden well knows; and we profess and declare it to you as the Vicar of Christ and to all Christendom.

But if your Holiness puts too much faith in the tales the English tell and will not give sincere belief to all this, nor refrain from favouring them to our prejudice, then the slaughter of bodies, the perdition of souls, and all the other misfortunes that will follow, inflicted by them on us and by us on them, will, we believe, be surely laid by the Most High to your charge.

To conclude, we are and shall ever be, as far as duty calls us, ready to do your will in all things, as obedient sons to you as His Vicar; and to Him as the Supreme King and Judge we commit the maintenance of our cause, casting our cares upon Him and firmly trusting that He will inspire us with courage and bring our enemies to nought.

May the Most High preserve you to His Holy Church in holiness and health and grant you length of days.

GIVEN at the monastery of Arbroath in Scotland on the sixth day of the month of April in the year of grace thirteen hundred and twenty and the fifteenth year of the reign of our King aforesaid.

Additional names inscribed on some of the seal tags: Alexander de Lambertoun★, Edwardus de Keth★, Johannes de Inchmertyn★, Thomas de Meiners★, Johannes Duraunt★, Thomas de Morham (and one illegible)★.

Endorsed: Littere directe ad dominum Supremum Pontificem per communitatem Scocie.

Additional names written on some of the seal tags: Alexander Lamberton★, Edward Keith★, John Inchmartin★, Thomas Menzies★, John Durrant★, Thomas Morham (and one illegible★).

Endorsed: Letter directed to our Lord the Supreme Pontiff by the community of Scotland.

IN THE SPRING of the year 1320 England and Scotland had been at war for just about twenty-three years. Only middle-aged and elderly people in Scotland could remember with any clarity the peaceful and prosperous reign of King Alexander III when the two countries had been living in amity time out of mind. That tranquillity had been shattered by the ambition of King Edward I, spurred by the opportunity, on Alexander's accidental death in 1286, of a Scotland suddenly weakened and leaderless. He had contrived to reduce it to the state of a vassal kingdom and soon afterwards to dethrone its king, John Balliol, and annex the realm. In early 1297 the Scots had revolted, first under the leadership of a junta of nobles and a brilliant guerrilla captain, Sir William Wallace, later under Robert Bruce, Earl of Carrick, who had the best claim to the vacant crown after King John and assumed it in 1306, the year before King Edward died. Against his much less able son King Edward II King Robert had steadily won back the kingdom in years of determined and skilful fighting, culminating in the destruction at Bannockburn in 1314 of the greatest army ever brought against him.

But Bannockburn had not ended the War of Independence. Its tide, none the less, was now running in the Scots' favour. In March 1318 they had at length won back the last English holding on Scottish soil, the once important town of Berwick-on-Tweed, now, after years of bitter warfare, reduced to little more than a frontier post, and its castle. They had then invaded England in their turn and devastated its northern counties. In 1319 they had held Berwick against a powerful English counter-attack, had swept over the Border again and on 20 September had routed an ill-found English army at the battle of Mytton in Yorkshire. At Christmas a truce had been arranged. It was to last for two years from 31 December 1319.[1]

But the war was not over. It was shifting from the military to the diplomatic field, where England carried more weight than Scotland. Pope Boniface VIII, who had been a good friend and ally to the Scots, had died in 1303, since when Papal policy had changed. Boniface's successors, Clement V and John XXII, both favoured King Edward II. Pope John, though less positively pro-English than the Gascon Clement, clearly regarded the Scots as trouble-some and as preventing the English by their persistent recalci-trance from joining in a crusade against the Turks. In 1317, the year after his elevation, he had despatched letters urging the con-clusion of peace to King Robert, who, since they were not addressed to him as a king, refused to read them. Relations with the Pope at Avignon were still strained. He had placed Scotland under an interdict and in November 1319 had summoned four Scottish bishops to appear at the Papal Court.[2]

It was time for a diplomatic counter-stroke, and in the spring of 1320 the memorable letter to the Pope generally known from its dating clause as the Declaration of Arbroath was composed and despatched to Avignon. Though its text has already been given it is worth summarizing at this point. It is an appeal to the Pope to use his influence justly and lays the whole of the Anglo-Scottish controversy before him as the Scots saw it, succinctly, with masterly persuasiveness and with an eloquence which sets it above all the diplomatic correspondence of the age. It starts with fundamentals, going back not merely to the origin of the war but to that of the Scottish nation itself—remote, romantic, partly legendary, partly imaginary—emphasizing that it has long been both a devoutly Christian nation and a free one. It summarizes King Edward I's treacherous attack on Scottish independence after, on the death of little Queen Margaret in 1290, the Scots found their ancient royal line broken and the crown in dispute among numerous claimants. Then, leaping over the interregnum and the brief reign of King John as an English puppet, the Letter dwells, accurately enough, on the sufferings of a country invaded and savagely devastated over and over again by the armies of Edward I and then Edward II. It next declares that the Scots have now got the upper hand through the leadership of their chosen and rightful king, to whom they pledge their gratitude and loyalty, but not yet complete victory; and in the most deeply felt passage of all proclaims their resolve, whether under that king or any other, to fight for their freedom to the death.

The Letter then turns to the state of Christendom, hard pressed by the Saracens, and declares the readiness of the Scottish king and people, unlike more self-seeking Christian kingdoms, to join in a Crusade—if only the Pope will use his influence to secure them honourable peace by reproving instead of supporting the English king. Finally the Letter calls on the Pope himself to remember his responsibilities as the Vicar of Christ and solemnly appeals over his head to that supreme King and Judge before bidding him a courteous farewell.

Our appreciation of the circumstances in which this memorable Letter was drawn up has till quite recently rested on the account of it given by Walter Bower, Abbot of Inchcolm, a small monastery on an island in the Firth of Forth, when writing, about a century and a half later, the first full-length history of Scotland, *Scotichronicon*, based on the *Gesta Annalia* of another cleric, John of Fordun, who wrote towards the end of the fourteenth century. Fordun's somewhat skeletal annals tell us nothing whatever of the Letter. But Bower tells us circumstantially that two Papal Legates arrived in Berwick, charged with a mission to King Robert, on 17 March 1320. 'On hearing of it,' says Bower, 'the magnates of the realm convened their assembly at the monastery of Arbroath, and by unanimous agreement wrote to the Supreme Pontiff, in haste to forestall the legates.' He then gives the text of the Letter as known to him. But it looks as if this circumstantial statement is merely Bower's deduction from the text of the Letter before him and from that of John of Fordun's *Gesta Annalia* which he was editing. Fordun did not know of the Declaration or he would surely have mentioned it. His terse narrative describes the 'Black Parliament' of August 1320 at which a conspiracy against King Robert was suppressed, and then adds: 'In the same year, on 17 March, legates of our Lord the Pope came to the King of Scotland at Berwick.'[3] Bower took 'the same year' to be 1320 and the legates' arrival therefore to have happened five months before the Black Parliament and three weeks before the date of the Letter, which led him to insert the phrases 'on hearing of this' and 'in haste to forestall the legates'. But Bower went astray in his chronology. According to the calendar used by Fordun, and indeed by Bower himself, the year did not begin till 25 March. The legates' arrival 'in the same year' therefore was not till 17 March 1320-1, nearly a year *after* the date of the Letter, and they were probably the Bishop of Winchester and the Bishop-elect of Vienne, whose fruitless mission King Edward II described in a letter to the Pope of 14 May 1321.[4]

The legates' arrival, then, did not precipitate the drafting of the Letter, as Bower asserted. It could have been done at leisure, with ample time to summon an assembly of the Scottish magnates to consider, approve and seal it. Modern historians agree with the suggestion of George Crawfurd in 1726[5] that it was probably composed by the Chancellor, Bernard de Linton, the Abbot of Arbroath; and its draft text, as I shall show, contained a distinct piece of evidence to support it. Moreover, the letter's unity of argument and style, as well as its art and scholarship, stamp it as the conception of a single and very able mind. It is quite possible, nevertheless, that there was some deliberation on the general terms of the Letter before it was drafted, and that the draft was also discussed before it was finally approved and sealed. It seems most probable that for the final discussion and sealing a full assembly of the magnates was held during the first week of April 1320.

For long it was assumed that they had met at Arbroath in a Parliament, and the Letter has been officially printed as an Act —the only Act—of that Parliament.[6] But modern historians have pointed out that beyond the Letter itself there is no evidence at all that any Parliament met at Arbroath in 1320; and even Bower does not say it did nor use the word *parliamentum*. The assembly of magnates who sealed the Letter did not include, as a Parliament would, any clerics; nor is there mention of any representatives from the burghs, although it is now recognized that such representatives were attending Scottish Parliaments long before the formerly accepted date of 1326.[7] This was a gathering of nobles and barons only.

But Professor G. W. S. Barrow, the most recent commentator on the Arbroath Declaration, thinks it possible that no final assembly was necessary and that 'the letter was in fact a round-robin', completed after preliminary deliberations, of which copies were 'sent round the country to as many of the nobles as possible' who 'would then make arrangements to have their seals attached to the final copies, of which there were at least two, and probably more'. He cites an English precedent of 1301.[8]

This theory seems to me to involve difficulties. Either the two parchments would have had to be carried to many different parts of the country—even though some of the lords may have been with the King and so readily accessible—which would risk the damage or loss of the documents and consequent delay; or a number of the magnates must have had to be induced to part with their private seals to send them to the Chancery. Although a great noble might do this, sending his seal in charge of a trusted deputy or a notary, it seems as unlikely a concession in an ordinary man as it would be to-day to part with his cheque-book with every blank cheque signed.

It is surely easier to suppose a special assembly to which the lords were summoned and, whether or not they had assisted at preliminary discussions, heard the document read over and agreed to put their seals to it.

But where did they meet? The accepted belief that they gathered at the monastery of Arbroath must be questioned. It can hardly be doubted that the last act took place in presence of the King, who is unlikely to have had his headquarters at a place so remote from the seat of war. True, it was the ordinary residence of his Chancellor; but for the important deliberations already supposed, and for the final act, the Chancellor, like the other officers of state, must surely have been with the King wherever he was.

According to the dating of writs issued in the King's name at this time, he was in Berwick on 25 and 26 March and 1 and 17 April, a long way from Arbroath. But it is possible that these datings were simply for reasons of propaganda, emphasizing that this Scottish town was again in Scottish hands, in the same way as Wallace and Moray in 1297 dated their famous letter to the Hanseatic authorities from the recovered Lothian town of Haddington.

Moreover, although the King may be supposed, *prima facie*, to have been at the place from which some writ of his was dated, Professor A. A. M. Duncan has demonstrated that that was not necessarily so. 'The *acta* do not reflect the movements of the king. . . . The exact dates of the king's presence at any one place can never be derived from the dating clauses of his *acta*.' Moreover the dating of *acta* from Arbroath, whose abbot was the Chancellor, merely shows that 'an itinerant chancery issued them at the direction of the chancellor who was there, or was conventionally said to be there'.[9]

We cannot be certain, then, that the Scottish magnates assembled at Arbroath—nor, for that matter, at Berwick. Either place, on the farthest eastern edge of the country, seems inconvenient. Some reasonably central place of meeting would be preferable, and it would probably be, like those of King Robert's Parliaments, at some monastery since its buildings would offer either the convent church itself or some hall large enough for meeting and debate, and also means for lodging a numerous and distinguished company and its attendants. Now the Chancery was apparently at Newbattle Abbey in Midlothian on 31 March,[10] and for this there is no obvious explanation except that the Chancellor was perhaps staying there. At this important juncture King and Chancellor were presumably together. I therefore tentatively suggest Newbattle Abbey as the place of the assembly of the magnates.

For Newbattle seems at this period to have been regarded as a convenient place, even for people who did not live in its neighbourhood, to visit for the transaction of business. An inquest ordered by the mayor and bailies of Berwick was held there on 25 June 1321;[11] and a dispute over marches between the monks of Dunfermline and the tenants of Leslie was discussed by arbiters who met at Newbattle on 13 March 1319–20,[12] only three weeks before the date of the Declaration of Arbroath. It may be significant that two of these arbiters, Sir David Wemyss and Alexander Lamberton, put their seals to the Declaration.[13] Was an assembly which included them already discussing it at Newbattle or just about to do so?

The people of Arbroath have long taken a justifiable pride in their town's association with the famous Letter to the Pope. It is traditionally called the Declaration of Arbroath and probably always will be: fitly enough if, as I believe, it was at least drafted in that abbey. But the exact place of its adoption is comparatively unimportant. It is of much greater interest to try to look into the minds of the men who adopted it and set their seals to it and of the anonymous genius who composed it, and to see how far we can accept Bower's statements that they wrote 'in haste', but 'with unanimous consent'.

Let us see, then, what light is to be found in the text, or texts, of the momentous document which they had gathered to approve.

---

[1] *Calendar of Documents relating to Scotland*, iii, no. 681; *Chron. de Lanercost*, p. 240.

[2] *Calendar of Papal Letters*, ii, p. 191.

[3] *Gesta Annalia*, cxxxv, ed. Skene (*The Historians of Scotland*, i, p. 349).

[4] *Foedera*, iii, p. 884.

[5] *The Lives and Characters of the Officers of the Crown and of the State in Scotland*, 1726, p. 18.

[6] *Acts of the Parliaments of Scotland*, i, pp. 474–5.

[7] G. W. S. Barrow: *Robert Bruce and the Community of the Realm of Scotland* (1965), p. 421.

[8] Barrow, pp. 424–5.

[9] *Scottish Historical Review*, xxxii, pp. 13–15, 30.

[10] *Ibid.*, p. 30.

[11] *Registrum de Neubotle*, p. 155.

[12] *Registrum de Dunfermelyn*, p. 239.

[13] Sir John Inchmartin, who was another of the original sixteen arbiters (*ibid.*), though not present at their Newbattle meeting, also put his seal to the Declaration.

2

THE TEXT OF THE DECLARATION I.

BERNARD DE LINTON.

THE TEXT OF THE DECLARATION II.

HISTORIANS AND EDITORS.

THE DECLARATION once existed in at least three versions: the draft, the final Letter sent to and received by the Pope at Avignon, and the copy of it preserved in Scotland. Of the three documents only the last has survived. It was in virtually perfect condition at the beginning of the eighteenth century, during the course of which it suffered, through damp, damage which destroyed parts of its text. But fortunately a most careful facsimile, engraved for the industrious and patriotic antiquary James Anderson and published after his death in his *Diplomata*,[1] has preserved for us its whole text but for two words perished in a fold of the parchment.

There has been much speculation about this document, long kept in the Earl of Haddington's house of Tyninghame and since 1829 in Her Majesty's General Register House. It has been thought to be the true original, which for some reason was not sent to the Pope, or of which the Pope received a duplicate or even merely a notarial instrument reciting the text. But we know that the Pope did receive the Letter, since he acknowledged having done so and, however feebly, acted upon it; and it is surely unthinkable that he could be expected to be impressed, as impressed he was, by anything but the original, authenticated by the actual seals of those in whose name it was addressed to him. More reasonably, the document has been regarded as a duplicate made for the purpose of record, a file copy. But even this explanation of its presence in Scotland raises two questions about it. It is surprising that a file copy should be sealed: the text, duly certified, should have been enough. And it is also remarkable that a file copy should contain so many mistakes, far more than have been hitherto detected.

This last fact may serve as the starting-point for an attempt to establish the correct text of the document sent to the Pope. Editors have long recognized that at two points it is necessary, to make sense, to import a word from the text of the Letter printed by Walter Goodall in his edition (still the only one) of Walter Bower's *Scotichronicon*, published in 1759: *vocacione* in line 13 where St Andrew is called 'the first of the Apostles *by calling* although second or third in rank', and *parati* in line 31 where the petitioners describe themselves as '*ready* to do your pleasure in all things'.[2] In borrowing these words from Goodall's text they cannot have failed to notice that he gives in a footnote a phrase from manuscripts of the *Scotichronicon* which does not appear in our document's text, and also adds after the name of Henry de St Clair the designation *panetarius Scotiae*, 'Pantler of Scotland', to which St Clair was in fact not entitled. Yet no editor has looked at the *Scotichronicon* manuscripts to find out what kind of text of the Letter they contain and how far Goodall followed it.

Since this simple fact struck me I have collated the text of the document formerly at Tyninghame with that in the five oldest *Scotichronicon* manuscripts—three in Edinburgh, one in London, and one in Cambridge. The search proved rewarding. The verbal differences between the manuscripts, including those due to carelessness or misreading by the scribes who copied them, are almost innumerable; but among them I reckon that the *Scotichronicon* text contains twenty-seven important variants from our document and sixteen of minor interest. These show that Walter Bower, writing in the middle of the fifteenth century, had before him a different document from that which we now possess; that all five manuscripts of the *Scotichronicon* contain substantially a copy of it; and that Goodall did not reproduce it. What Goodall did was to transcribe the facsimile in Anderson's *Diplomata*, evidently regarding its original as the only authentic text, and use the manuscripts before him only for a very few amendments and the gloss already mentioned.

I now feel certain that what Bower had before him was the draft of the Letter, and that from a comparison of it (which for brevity I will call Sc) with the Tyninghame manuscript (Tyn) it is possible to reconstruct a text approximating very closely to that which went to Avignon. Further, from a study of both versions I think some new light can be thrown on the manner and circumstances in which the Letter was composed, revised, and sealed.

To begin with, wherever the assembly of the magnates was held, comparison of the texts suggests that there was some difficulty in collecting them all together. When the draft was prepared, thirty-six names were listed in the opening lines of the Letter—those of barons who had either appeared or, having been summoned, were confidently expected. But one prominent baron who must have been expected was missing—the young Sir Andrew de Moray, lord of Bothwell. The son of Wallace's fellow commander at the battle of Stirling Bridge, he was one of the King's most active supporters, and five years later married his twice-widowed sister, Lady Christian

Bruce.[3] Either the official messengers had not reached him or else he was ill—but he did not send his seal. It was he who was the hereditary Pantler of Scotland, and the draft must at first have contained his name among the rest—*Andreas de Moravia panetarius Scocie*. When he failed to appear his name was struck through, but not his designation (though that was eliminated in the final copy), so that in the document transcribed by Bower the words *panetarius Scocie* survived and seemed to be attached to the previous name, that of Henry de St Clair; and Goodall so incorporated them in his edition of the *Scotichronicon*.

But though Moray was absent, three other magnates arrived before the final version of the Letter was penned—or, if already present, were persuaded to the inclusion of their names, which are not in the draft. They were Roger de Moubray, William Olifaunt, and William de Montealto (Mowat). But even now seven more barons were still absent—or still reluctant. Their names were added last of all. They could not be written into the document that was to go to the Pope nor into the file copy: both were already complete. They were written on the extra tags by which their seals, like their predecessors', were attached to the two parchments.

Professor Barrow hints that not all the participants were really willing, since in the Black Parliament held at Scone in the following August five of them were accused and three convicted of treason, apparently involved in a plot to replace King Robert on the throne by William de Soules, whose name stands tenth in the list and who was the son of a former Competitor for the Crown. It may be significant that of the three men whose names were not in the draft and included only in the final copy one, Roger de Moubray, was convicted of treason in the Black Parliament, and another, William Olifaunt, although he had taken part in the gallant defence of Stirling Castle against King Edward I in 1303–4, had later, as a prisoner of war, spent nine years in England.

These coincidences seem to support Professor Barrow's suggestion that 'some of the magnates had been deliberately chosen to seal the document as a test of their loyalty and future intentions'.[4] One such may well have been the Earl of March, who at one time had been, like his father, an English partisan, and who had received and sheltered King Edward II, when a fugitive from the field of Bannockburn, in his castle of Dunbar. I think this theory is further strengthened by Tyn's outstanding feature—its inaccuracy. It is perfectly plain that this copy was written out in great haste, and for this I can think of only one explanation: the need for it was sudden—and unexpected.

The signs of haste are not superficially apparent. The document is a superb piece of penmanship and the writing is neat and regular. There are no deletions or corrections anywhere. But their absence proves that the copy cannot have been collated with the original nor even read over after it was finished. If it had been, the scribe must have realized its many errors, including the omission of *vocacione* and *parati* already mentioned and furthermore (as no editor has noticed) of a *cum* in line 23 essential to the construction. Many other errors will be discussed later. They all suggest that the writer of the file copy was not the man who had penned the original.

In only one way can I account for the obvious haste with which some clerk, with impatient men standing over him, wrote out the only contemporary manuscript of the Arbroath Declaration that we now possess. The Chancellor, or some other principal figure, perhaps even the King himself, had suddenly thought it essential to preserve a *sealed* duplicate of the Letter as incontrovertible evidence of all the magnates' adherence to its terms. But time pressed. The unanimity achieved might waver. Some of the men who had been summoned may have been called from business on their estates to which they were anxious to return. There had perhaps been argument to protract the assembly and it was impatient to disperse. But all the seals already applied to the Letter must without exception be applied to the duplicate, and till that moment no duplicate had been contemplated.

Hastily, then, a clerk wrote one out. The agreed Letter was not dictated to him: he had it beside him, and as he glanced to and fro his eye occasionally missed or transposed a word. No sooner had he finished than the parchment was snatched up for the slitting and insertion of the seal-tags. It was perhaps at this very moment that the seven missing barons arrived. Their late appearance may be evidence that Bower had after all some authority for his statement that the whole transaction was carried through 'in haste'.

But the Letter itself was not composed in haste. It was not drafted at the same time and place as the assembly of magnates, for if it had been the writer would have known more precisely who was present. On the other hand, the fact that the draft bears the same date as the final copy shows that it was written not more than two or three weeks in advance, for the writer knew the day for which the magnates had been summoned. In the short interval there was time for the draft to be amended, considered, and approved by the King and his Council before its presentation to the magnates.

But if, as seems probable, the unanimity that the Declaration expresses was not altogether wholehearted we cannot be sure what the difficulties were. Speculation is possible. Perhaps some of the magnates who had been partisans of King John resented the total exclusion of reference to him. For he, too, had suffered wrong. His claim to the Crown had been as good as King Robert's, indeed better: he, 'by the strict rule of primogeniture, was the true heir to the Crown and office of king'.[5] He had been duly, according to immemorial custom, set upon the royal stone at Scone—the last King of Scots to be so inaugurated there—had reigned as acknowledged sovereign, and had been unjustifiably and humiliatingly dethroned by the English usurper. He had left two lawful sons (one of whom did in fact claim the Scottish Crown with English help twelve years later). King Robert as yet had none, and, as later events of this very year were to show, did not command the sincere allegiance of all the magnates now assembled.

Some no doubt were weary of the war, but others, to whom fighting was no disagreeable occupation and who had no thought for its drain upon their country's resources, did not perhaps object to its dragging on. They may have had no wish to appeal to the Pope. Others again may have deprecated the boldness with which, despite its courtesy, the Letter addressed the Vicar of Christ on earth.

Moreover, there were certainly many prominent men who might have been expected to seal the Letter but did not; and no historian, I think, has hitherto considered them except Professor Barrow.[6] On his theory, we might have expected to find the seal of Walter FitzGilbert, who, though he joined King Robert after Bannockburn, had at the time of that battle been holding Bothwell Castle for the English; of Sir William Carlyle who had turned to what had become the winning side only in 1317, and of Sir Thomas Colville who had done so as recently as 1319.

But on the other hand there could be no suspicion of the loyalty of many whose seals were also not added. The absence of Sir Andrew de Moray, already mentioned, is no more surprising than that of Nicholas Scrymgeour, whose father, like Sir Andrew's, had been a comrade of Wallace's and whom King Robert was to confirm in 1324 in that father's office of standard-bearer. The fidelity of both is unquestionable. So is that of Sir Malcolm Fleming, the

Sheriff of Dumbarton, of Sir Duncan Campbell of Loudoun, Sheriff of Ayr, of Sir Alan Cathcart, Sir Robert Boyd and Sir Robert Rutherfurd, all veterans of the war since its darkest days, of Patrick Ogilvy, John Elphinstone, Sir Andrew Gray and Henry Maule. They cannot all have been prevented by sickness; nor can the absence of them all from the place of assembly be explained by distance, as may that of Angus Og, Lord of the Isles, of Kenneth Mackenzie, and of Sir Colin Campbell of Lochow—who was, however, represented by Donald Campbell, his uncle. Strange, too, is the absence of Sir Adam de Gordon, a Berwickshire magnate, who was subsequently one of the two messengers entrusted with the precious document to carry it to Avignon.

Perhaps there is no single explanation of all these discrepancies. It is only clear that a baron's loyalty is neither made certain by his presence in the assembly nor dubious by his absence. The facts are probably that the organizers of the Declaration collected a quite sufficiently imposing body of supporters, impressed a few more as an afterthought and were joined by a few more as volunteers. The number included eight earls and the tutor or guardian of a ninth, and all the Officers of State or of the Household who were laymen except the Pantler: Sir Alexander Fraser was, though not so designated, the Chamberlain.

But that there was misgiving and hesitation among a minority is suggested by the tardy inclusion of some names and by the sinister sequel of the Black Parliament. It is also suggested by the fact that a sealed duplicate of the Letter, plainly prepared in haste, was preserved. Such a duplicate, apart from an ordinary official record, was most unusual—though Professor Gordon Donaldson has cited an almost contemporary example in England.[7]

We do not have to speculate, however, on what happened to the original Letter after the assembly had dispersed. Two knights travelled with it to Avignon, bearing also a letter to the Pope from the King which has not survived. They were Sir Edward de Maubuisson and Sir Adam de Gordon. Of the former nothing seems to be known. The latter had been by no means a Bruce partisan in earlier days, but he had been received into favour after Bannockburn and he had had diplomatic experience.

The envoys either had some difficulty, from adverse weather or from the danger of English ships, in making their way to France or it took them some time, after reaching Avignon, to gain an audience with the Pope. A narrative explaining the delay is in print, but lacks any documentary support.[8] The Pope cannot have received the Letter by 16 June, on which date he excommunicated the King again as well as the Scottish bishops who had ignored their summons to Avignon, nor even as late as 29 July, when he addressed a letter to King Robert urging him to make peace with the English and excusing himself for not addressing him as King of Scots but merely as one 'calling himself King of Scotland and acting as King'.[9] The Papal letter gives no indication whatever of any communication's having arrived from Scotland.

There is one possible explanation of the striking gap between 6 April, the date of the Letter, and the first evidence of the Pope's having read it—that the messengers did not leave Scotland till well after midsummer. If this was so, how could such a delay be in turn explained? It is not likely that the assembly of the magnates did not take place till June or July, for in that case the April date on the draft could hardly have been allowed to stand unaltered. The probability is that 6 April is the true date of the assembly and that some unforeseen circumstance delayed not the messengers' departure but their arrival.

Very soon after 29 July, at any rate, the Scottish envoys must have been received, for on 10 August the Pope wrote, as the message they brought asked him to do, to King Edward II, urging him to conclude peace with the Scots and describing the horrors of war in almost the very phrases he had read in the Scots' letter— 'slaughter of bodies, perdition of souls, wasting of goods and other misfortunes not easily to be named'.[10]

Six days later, on 16 August, the Pope wrote to King Robert to say that he had received and listened to the two knights, whom he named. He still addressed the King in the same cautious style and again exhorted him to make peace, but he indicated his favour by granting him a suspension of the sentence of excommunication under which he lay. This letter, too, recalled phrases from the Declaration, acknowledging that previous Popes had 'distinguished that kingdom and its kings with many privileges'. On the same day the Pope addressed a mild exhortation to the Bishop of St Andrews.[11]

Finally, on 28 August, the Pope formally and courteously acknowledged receipt of the Declaration itself, addressing his letter to the Scottish earls named in it, the Butler, Constable and Marischal, 'and many other noble men of the said kingdom'. Understanding that the King of England and 'the said Robert' were contemplating negotiations, he adjured the magnates of Scotland to turn their minds towards concord and unity. To the main petition in their letter he sent no direct answer, but the same day he drew up the outlines of an Anglo-Scottish truce and also wrote again to King Edward, informing him of his discussions with the Scottish envoys and also of the suspension of King Robert's sentence of excommunication.[12]

These non-committal Papal gestures did nothing whatever to hasten the end of the war, which broke out again after the 1319 truce was ended; but they show that the Declaration and its memorable language made no little impression on Pope John's mind and convinced him at least that there was another side to the controversy than that displayed to him by English propaganda. It took him, however, another three and a half years to bring himself to accord King Robert his proper style and title.

It was not till 1328 that King Edward III formally recognized King Robert's title and the independence of Scotland, and the Treaty of Northampton, a year before King Robert's death, brought the long struggle of more than thirty years to a close.

To point out that the Declaration of Arbroath had little practical effect, and even to endorse the suggestion that there may not have been complete unanimity behind it, is emphatically not to doubt or impugn its pre-eminent character as an expression of patriotism. True, it had a kind of precedent, as a recent writer has pointed out, in a remonstrance addressed to the same Pope in 1318 by Donald O'Neill and other chiefs of Ireland, protesting against English rule and declaring their support for King Robert's brother Edward Bruce as High King of Ireland.[13] But that verbose document offers no parallel to the controlled passion of the Arbroath Declaration which stands out, both in its own time and in the perspective of history, as one of the loftiest statements ever penned of a nation's claim to freedom. Yet scarcely any people in history has been genuinely unanimous on any subject without some minority of dissidents, doubters, or dastards. Its leaders have spoken for it, gathering up and voicing the highest sentiments of which the majority is capable. So it was in Scotland in 1320. 'Here is not a description of the patriotism that actually existed in Bruce's Scotland but an idealized picture of the patriotism conceived in the minds of those closest to Bruce',[14] and chiefly in the mind of the great Abbot of Arbroath, his Chancellor.

It is important to recognize this leadership behind the Letter which voices for all time the claim of small nations to be free from aggression by great ones. It came from no Parliament, nor any other kind of national assembly; yet its signatories spoke, in their own words, for 'the other barons and freeholders and the whole community of the realm'.

By many the last phrase has been sentimentally treasured as signifying the mass of the people, even an emergent democracy: the earliest English translation of the Letter, in 1689 (see below, p. 40), rendered *tota Communitas* as 'the whole community, or commons'. But the *communitas* was not the commonalty. It was the body which, at Norham in 1291, refused to accept Edward I's claim to suzerainty over Scotland, in a polite but firm reply discovered and printed by Professor Lionel Stones in 1956: '*les hauts hommes d'Escoce*'—in Professor Barrow's phrase 'the responsible men'—to whom the commonalty looked for leadership and a voice.[15]

This was the *communitas* for which the eight earls and thirty-eight barons spoke. To them the King's nearest and most loyal councillors presented for their adoption the Letter stating Scotland's right and Scotland's resolution in terms which express a new-born sense of nationhood. And among those councillors was the man who, recalling the sufferings and struggles of the whole people and trusting them even to the last hundred men, could put those aspirations into such splendid words.

---

[1] *Selectus Diplomatum et Numismatum Scotiae Thesaurus*, 1739, no. LI.
[2] For these and other line-references see the variorum text at the end of the book.
[3] *Scots Peerage*, ii, pp. 127–8.
[4] Barrow, *op. cit.*, p. 429.
[5] Barrow, p. 56, and authorities there cited.
[6] Barrow, p. 430.
[7] *Scottish Historical Review*, xxix, p. 119.
[8] *Records of Aboyne* (New Spalding Club), pp. 361–2.
[9] Theiner, *Vetera Monumenta*, no. 429.
[10] *Ibid.*, no. 430.
[11] *Ibid.*, nos. 431–2.
[12] *Ibid.*, nos. 433–5. Professor Donaldson has published a translation of the Pope's reply (*S.H.R.*, xxix, pp. 119–20).
[13] *Scotichronicon*, ii, pp. 259–67; Ranald Nicholson: 'Magna Carta and the Declaration of Arbroath', in *University of Edinburgh Journal*, 1965, p. 143.
[14] Nicholson, *loc. cit.*, p. 144.
[15] *S.H.R.*, xxxv, pp. 108–9; Barrow, pp. 43–6.

BERNARD DE LINTON

THE SHORT LIST of famous Scotsmen known to the man in the street does not include Abbot Bernard de Linton. In justice it should. The unflinching patriotism, the lofty sentiment, the stirring and memorable language of the Declaration of Arbroath have long been credited to the men in whose names it stands. But these attributes, if there was dissension or hesitation among the nobles and barons, belong primarily to the man who drew up the Declaration, though his own name is not in it, and who no doubt did most to persuade them to accept and seal it. A great man and great leader has stood too long in the shadows of history and the light of glory should reach him. To him, not alone but principally, is due the admiration of those who read this immortal document. His abbey of Arbroath, whose noble ruins are today visited by many, may not have held the assembly that sealed the Declaration; but almost certainly the draft of that document was composed and first written down within its walls.

For two and a half centuries it has been generally agreed that Bernard de Linton was probably the actual composer of the Declaration. Yet he still remains a remote and shadowy figure. He is never mentioned in Barbour's *The Brus*. Professor Barrow calls him 'one of the really outstanding mediaeval royal chancellors', and Lord Cooper declared, 'Someone ought to write Bernard's biography.'[1] Only George Crawfurd in his *Officers of State* has given a sketch of it, very superficial and full of errors; and the plain fact is that the materials are sadly scanty.

Nothing is known of Bernard's origins. Professor Barrow assumes that he took his name from one or other of the parishes in southern Scotland named Linton, and Crawfurd suggested that he sprang from a landed family of that name. This is quite likely, since three Lintons besides himself were prominent enough to be found on the 'Ragman Roll', one of them, Philip de Linton, having been constable of Berwick in 1291.[2]

Bernard's first recorded appearance is in this melancholy company, among those obliged to swear allegiance to King Edward I at Berwick, on 28 August 1296. He was then a parish priest, at Mordington, four miles from Berwick—'Bernard de Lyntone, persone del eglise de Mordingtone'. He must have known much—

he may even have himself witnessed something—of King Edward's appalling sack of Berwick and slaughter of its people earlier in the year. Those horrors could have turned any man from a peaceful and scholarly cleric, if such he was, into a determined and un-wearying labourer for his country's freedom. Bernard's words in the Declaration of Arbroath that no one could describe or even imagine the English atrocities in Scotland who had not seen them himself have the ring of personal experience.

Nothing else is known of his career before King Robert's coronation in 1306, but he must have become prominent among the patriotic clergy during the early years of the struggle for independence or he could not, so suddenly after the beginning of the reign, have been raised to high office. It is tempting to suppose a friendship between Bernard and Nicholas de Balmyle, a canon of Dunblane. Nicholas was 'one of the handful of key men who directed the national struggle' in 1301 when he was Chancellor of Scotland, appointed by the Guardians of the Kingdom in name of King John;[3] and he became Bishop of Dunblane in 1307. He was one of the bishops who, at a Parliament held in St Andrews in March 1309, formally declared their support for King Robert, and reiterated it at Dundee a year afterwards and again in about 1314,[4] thus setting one precedent for the laymen's declaration of 1320. If Bernard was intimate with Nicholas he could have learnt something of the workings of the Chancery and conceivably have accompanied the bishop-elect to Avignon. One way or another, he must have attained prominence among Robert Bruce's supporters, for the King appointed him to be his Chancellor very soon after his coronation. The first actual reference to Bernard as Chancellor is on 14 October 1308.[5] By 1311 he had become Abbot of Arbroath, from the revenues of which Nicholas's salary as Chancellor had been paid.

From 1308 Bernard de Linton is prominent almost throughout King Robert's reign, holding the office of Chancellor and clearly enjoying the King's highest confidence. Once at least he went abroad, sailing to Norway on the King's business, very likely to negotiate the treaty between Scotland and Norway concluded in 1312.[6]

Lord Cooper has drawn attention to the fact that five other state papers of the reign are also written in the formal and musical prose of the *ars dictaminis* and suggested that they were 'written by the same hand or passed for revision under the same eye' as the Declaration of Arbroath. These are the magnates' letter to Philip the Fair, King of France, in 1309; the bishops' declaration in favour of King Robert at St Andrews and Dundee; the manifestos regarding the succession to the Crown in 1315 and 1318; and the peace terms of 1326. Lord Cooper points to the same insistence in all six documents on the horrors of war and the same style in each of reference to Almighty God by a quotation from the Vulgate adapted to fit a *cursus*. It does seem plausible to regard the great Chancellor as the author or drafter of all these documents which, from 1309 to 1326, all fall within his term of office. The only other work ascribed to him is a Latin poem on the battle of Bannockburn of which several passages are quoted by Bower.[7] He may have been correct in crediting these awkward hexameters to Abbot Bernard, but I hope not.

In 1327 Bernard was elected Bishop of Sodor or the Isles, the King granting him £100 towards the expenses of his election,[8] and consecrated the following year. He was still Chancellor in early 1328,[9] but was not so styled on 13 November of that year when he witnessed a royal charter as Bishop of Sodor.[10] His retirement would be natural, for unless he was an extremely young parson in 1296 he must have been several years older than the King he had served so faithfully, who died in 1329 at the age of 55. Perhaps the reward of his long service by only this poor and obscure bishopric is less surprising than it looks, and attributable either to his age and infirmity, unequal to the administration of a great diocese, or to the modesty with which Crawfurd credits him. Modesty would be consistent with a character which seems to have left no record in popular tradition, since he is little noticed by Fordun or Bower and ignored by Barbour, who had known some of his contemporaries.

Bernard de Linton did not hold his bishopric for much more than three years. He died before May 1331, perhaps while on a journey to or from his see in the Isle of Man, for he was buried in the monastery of Kilwinning in Ayrshire, not far from the port of Irvine,[11] by monks of the same Tironensian order as his former brethren at Arbroath.

[1] Barrow, p. 253; Lord Cooper: *Supra Crepidam*, p. 54.
[2] *Calendar of Documents*, ii, pp. 138, 201, 207, 208, 213.
[3] Barrow, p. 169.
[4] Barrow, pp. 262, n. 4; *ibid.*, p. 379: *A.P.S.*, i, p. 460.
[5] Barrow, p. 253.
[6] *Liber S. Thome de Aberbrothoc*, 360.
[7] *Scotichronicon*, ii, pp. 148–50.
[8] *Exchequer Rolls*, i, p. 114.
[9] *Ibid.*, p. 59; *R.M.S.*, ii, 3717.
[10] Register House Charters, 95.
[11] Bishop John Dowden: *The Bishops of Scotland*, pp. 281–2.

Part of draft text of the Declaration, showing early version of one passage: '*non enim propter gloriam belli diuicias aut honores pugnamus sed propter leges paternas et libertatem solummodo . . .*' 'It is not in truth for the glory of war, riches or honours that we are fighting but for the laws of our fathers and for liberty alone . . .'

IT IS NOW time for a closer look at the text of the Declaration. I do not think that any discussion of it in March or April 1320 was concerned with amending the style. Essential differences between Sc and Tyn, when not obvious errors, seem to be the work of a single reviser, presumably the Chancellor himself, improving, polishing, and sharpening his own composition. Other differences are due to the haste with which the scribe of Tyn wrote.

I deal first with the signs of revision.

In lines 3, 5, and 6, as already mentioned, three names not in Sc have been inserted and *panetarius Scocie* has been deleted.

In line 8 the Scots, originally said to have emigrated 'from the confines of Greece and Egypt', as a Scottish propagandist of 1301 had maintained, are now said to have started from 'Greater Scythia', in order, as Professor Barrow points out, to strengthen their connection with their patron St Andrew, who traditionally preached to the Scythians.[1] This change was noted by Goodall.

In line 15 the former phrase *Eadwardus Rex Anglie* has been altered to *Rex Anglorum Edwardus*, presumably to bring *Edwardus* close to the next phrase *pater istius qui nunc est*—'the father of that (Edward) who now reigns', and also to make the rhythm of a *cursus planus*, the reason for which I shall explain in a moment.

In line 18 *velut* is changed to *quasi* to sharpen the comparison of King Robert to the heroes of the Old Testament.

In line 22 the resolution of *volumus* has been strengthened by putting *aliquatenus* before it instead of after it as in Sc. Then in the next sentence, containing the most famous passage of the whole Letter, only recently discovered to have been partly quoted from Sallust, occur the most striking of all the revisions. The draft had read, 'It is not for the glory *of war*, riches or honours that we fight, but for *the laws of our fathers and for* freedom alone.' In the terser final version we can surely discern the true stylist pruning the sentence to add to its force and leaving *solummodo*—'for that and that alone'—to emphasize the single word 'freedom' rather than a phrase.

In line 22 *Sanctissime* has been changed to *Reuerende*, no doubt for the sake of variety, since *Sanctissimus* appears, in one case or another, in three other passages of the Letter.

33

In line 23 the main appeal of the Letter has been fortified by adding the imploring words *genuflexis cordibus* to the draft.

In line 24 Tyn's *Regem* differs from the *regi* of three manuscripts of Sc and the *regis* of two others. Originally the sole verb was *monere*, needing a dative noun; but in revision a second verb was added—*monere et exhortari*—and the noun, yielding to *exhortari*, was changed to the accusative. We know that *exhortari* was in the Letter sent to the Pope from his quotation of this passage in his reply to it of 28 August.[2]

In line 30, too, an alteration is confirmed by the Pope, this time in his letter to King Edward of 10 August. The phrase in Sc, *animarum exterminia*, was strengthened to *animarum exicia* as in Tyn, and *animarum excicia* appears in a paraphrase of this passage in the Pope's letter, as Lord Hailes long ago pointed out.[3]

Finally, in the dating clause (line 32) appears a most significant revision. The Letter in Tyn bears to have been written 'at the monastery of Abirbrothoc', but Sc shows that the draft had read 'at *our* monastery of Abirbrothoc'. Automatically the Chancellor or his clerk had used the phrase habitual to an abbot issuing a charter or granting a tack; but the tell-tale *nostrum* was struck out in revision. Here surely is confirmatory evidence of Bernard de Linton's authorship of the Declaration.[4]

The other main group of differences comprises the slips of the copyist. In identifying these we are sometimes helped by knowing that the Letter is, as Lord Cooper pointed out, 'a practically fault-less specimen of the *ars dictaminis* of the thirteenth century' and moreover 'replete with apt quotations' from the Vulgate and from classical authors. Lord Cooper identified nine quotations from the Vulgate, each slightly altered in wording to accord with the rhythmical requirements of the *ars dictaminis*. The draft text in Sc reveals a tenth, spoiled in Tyn by the copyist's haste or possibly by his ignorance of this highly elaborate style.

The *ars dictaminis*, developed to its fullest in the Papal Curia of the thirteenth century, was used in five other state papers of Robert I's reign between 1309 and 1326, which as already noted may serve as contributory evidence for Bernard de Linton's author-ship of the Declaration of Arbroath, since he must have had a hand in framing all five. This style demanded that the *clausulae* or closing cadences of a phrase should be in one of three rhythms according to the sentiment of the context, the *cursus planus*, the *cursus tardus*, or the *cursus velox*. These were framed not, as in classical Latin, from the quantities of the vowels but from the accent of the words.

Lord Cooper gives as illustrations three English phrases:

Cursus Planus: dactyl-trochee—'servants departed'
Cursus Tardus: dactyl-dactyl—'perfect felicity'
Cursus Velox: dactyl-ditrochee—'glorious undertaking'

The skilful use of this intricate style, coming from a remote monastery of north-western Europe, in a country humbly named as 'poor little Scotland, beyond which there is no dwelling-place at all', must surely have impressed the Papal Curia and contributed to the Letter's effect as propaganda.[5]

We shall see how attention to the *clausulae* helps to identify some of Tyn's errors.

In line 9 the copyist abridged *ferocissimas gentes*—the 'savage races' among whom the primitive Scots had lived—to the weak *ferocissimos*, thereby destroying a *cursus planus*. Later in the same line he spoiled a *cursus velox* by omitting *gentibus*.

In line 10 he made likewise two errors. He omitted the three words *per mare rubrum*, so that instead of saying 'After the people of Israel crossed the Red Sea' the Letter cryptically reads 'After the people of Israel crossed'. He also misread *cum* as *sibi*, thereby repeating a word already given earlier in the sentence.

In line 12 there are also two errors. Where Sc shows that the author had worked in a phrase from Revelations—'King of kings and Lord of lords', transposing the *words dominus dominancium* to make a *cursus tardus*, the writer of Tyn has spoilt both the quotation and the *cursus* by omitting *dominancium*. Further, by transposing *suam* to follow *Resurreccionem* he has spoilt a *cursus velox*.

Line 13, as already mentioned, lacks the *vocacione* needed to explain St Andrew's position as *primum* and to balance *ordine*. In the same line I believe the unanimous *sanctum* of the Sc manuscripts, in every case abbreviated to *stm*, to have been miscopied by the scribe of Tyn, who in his haste wrote in error the abbreviation of *scilicet* instead of that of *sanctum*, thus changing the respectfully formal 'Saint Andrew' into 'to wit, Andrew'. When, in line 8, he really intended *scilicet* he wrote the word in full. The two earliest editors of Tyn, Bishop Gilbert Burnet and Sir George Mackenzie, preferred to read *sanctum*, and I think they were right.

All the early editors disliked the inelegant *Ita quod* of line 14 and read *Itaque* instead. Sc shows that the copyist's eye skipped the intervening word in the phrase *Ita quippe quod*.

Line 16 recites the atrocities committed in Scotland by Edward I in a long list of nouns which the copyist, apparently not expecting it, interrupted by inserting an *et*; and in line 17 he shortened the phrase 'besides other outrages *without number*', his eye perhaps jumping from one terminal—*a* to another over the words *enormia et innumera*.

In line 20 he omitted *nostro* and in line 21 *ex nobis*. The latter omission seriously weakens the resolute phrase 'So long as but a hundred *of us* remain alive'.

There are two errors in line 23. No editor has noticed that the subjunctive *sit* needs the governing conjunction *cum* which is given in Sc so as to read, '*Since* there is no weighing nor distinction with (Christ).' Further, the copyist has repeated the word *pondus*, writing *Pondus et pondus*. That reading makes sense of a kind; but much more effective, with only one *pondus*, are the three pairs of balanced nouns—'There is neither weighing nor distinction of Jew and Greek, Scotsman or Englishman'. The immaterial change of the last conjunction from the *vel* of Sc to the *aut* of Tyn may be either a revision or an error.

In line 26 the scribe of Tyn rendered *arctari indies* meaningless by writing *artari in dies*.

In line 31 he omitted, as already mentioned, the essential *parati* which Goodall restored (and Lord Cooper inadvertently inserted in the wrong place). In line 33, less seriously, he omitted the word *mensis* from the date.

There are other variants which may be due to either revision or hasty copying, but are equally acceptable, such as *prisce* or *priscorum* in line 11, *hactenus libera* or *libera hactenus* in line 15, and *refert* or *interest* in line 25; and *primo* in line 10, omitted by Tyn, is not essential.

---

[1] Barrow, p. 426; Eusebius, *Historiae Ecclesiasticae*, III. i. 1.

[2] Theiner, *Vetera Monumenta*, no. 433

[3] *Ibid.*, no. 430; Hailes's *Annals of Scotland*, ii, pp. 97–8.

[4] Abbot Bernard uses the *nostrum* only once in the dating of about a dozen writs in his name recorded in the *Liber S. Thome de Aberbrothoc*, in an assedation of 1325 (i, 352). But cf. the abbots of Melrose in 1316 —'*in monasterio nostro de Melros*' (*Liber de Calchou* i, p. 135), of Kelso in 1330—'*in monasterio nostro*'—and 1370—'*apud monasterium nostrum*' (*ibid.*, ii. pp. 377, 406), and of Dunfermline in 1328—'*apud sepefatum nostrum monasterium*' (*Registrum de Dunfermelyn*, p. 254), and many later instances down to the Reformation.

[5] *Supra Crepidam*, pp. 50–5.

FULL OF PROBLEMS as the text of the Declaration of Arbroath already is, it has been handled by most editors if not with positive carelessness at least with insufficient care. There is only one acceptably faithful transcription of Tyn, made a hundred years ago by Cosmo Innes for the *National Manuscripts of Scotland*—its sole error is to read *impugnata* for *inpugnata* in line 10: even the great Thomas Thomson made four mistakes. Earlier editors were either unskilled in palaeography or preferred their own spelling and grammar to that of 1320. Later ones did not read their proofs closely enough. But there have been so many editors and so many publications of the text as to dispose utterly of the modern myth that historians have ignored or even suppressed the Declaration.

Yet its bibliographical history has hardly been studied at all. In 1965 I sought information from three distinguished Scottish historians on when the famous Letter had first appeared in print and none could tell me, though one supplied the clue that led to the answer.

Of the three original manuscripts, that which the Scottish envoys carried to the Pope has never been found, either in Avignon or in Rome. The draft probably remained at Arbroath while Bernard de Linton was Chancellor and thereafter became part of the muniments of that abbey where Bower, who was the Abbot of Inchcolm, could have seen it. The file copy with its noble array of seals must have been placed with the national records, which were few in number and bulk at that time, since almost all those of earlier centuries had been carried off by Edward I twenty-four years before. It would thus come under the care of the Clerk of the Rolls—the learned and accomplished William de Irwyn in 1328[1] —and his successors as Clerk of the Rolls or Clerk Register, and be lodged in due course with the other public records in Edinburgh Castle, where the 'Register Hous' was in 1540.[2]

That it was preserved carefully its almost perfect condition four hundred years later clearly shows. Whether it was read in early Stewart times we cannot tell. Walter Bower, as we have seen, copied another version of it—but this may have been because he had examined the official copy and realized its imperfections. John Maitland, Lord Thirlestane, Chancellor of Scotland under James VI from 1586 till his death in 1595, seems to be echoing phrases from line 11 of the Declaration in some admonitory verses which he addressed to the Regent Mar in 1571, though the appearance may be fortuitous:

> Scotland cam never yet in servitude
> Sen Fergus First, bot ever has been free,
> And has been always bruikit [possessed] by ane blude
> And kin of kings, descendit gree by gree.[3]

But historians and other writers of that period make no mention of it. There is no allusion to it by George Buchanan, whose history of Scotland was anyway very little based on original documents,[4] nor by Sir John Skene, who was later stigmatized by Lord Hailes as 'a careless, if not an unfaithful publisher',[5] nor by the diligent Sir Robert Sibbald. Sir James Balfour of Denmylne, Lyon King of Arms under Charles I and Charles II, seems to be the first writer since Bower to allude to the Declaration of Arbroath. He left a brief account of it in his manuscript 'Annals', which, however, were not printed till the nineteenth century. It was only the constitutional aspect of it that interested him and he did not copy the text, but he did list the magnates in whose name the Letter was sent. His list shows that he read it in some manuscript of the *Scotichronicon*, not in the official copy, for he omits the names of Roger de Moubray, William Olifaunt, and William de Montealto which are not in the draft text (and also, by an oversight, that of Reginald le chen), and gives Henry de St Clair the mistaken designation of 'pantler of Scotland'.[6]

By Balfour's time the official copy was no longer in Edinburgh. In 1612 the Register House in the Castle was being repaired and improved, the work, in those enlightened days, being given priority over work urgently needed on other Government buildings. This was during the brief tenure of office as Clerk Register of Sir Thomas Hamilton of Byres, later 1st Earl of Haddington, an able lawyer and statesman and also a scholar and antiquary. His special interests, combined with his official duty to safeguard the public records from the dust and disturbance of the building operations, easily explain why he removed quantities of the records, including the Declaration of Arbroath, to his own house in East Lothian to study them at leisure.[7]

To this somewhat unorthodox action of Hamilton's we owe, first, some invaluable transcripts of large portions of the older records whose originals disappeared as a result of Cromwell's removal of almost all the public records to London, and secondly the survival of our contemporary copy of the Declaration of Arbroath which, it seems, Hamilton retained as a curiosity. The Earls of Haddington kept it at Tyninghame until 1829, though, it is clear, they readily made it available to scholars who desired to study and copy it.

The credit of printing the Declaration of Arbroath for the first time belongs to another learned man, Sir George Mackenzie of Rosehaugh, Lord Advocate under Charles II and founder of the Advocates' Library (now the National Library of Scotland). Among his thirty or so publications is his *Observations upon the Laws and Customs of Nations as to Precedency*, printed at Edinburgh in 1680. Its third chapter bears the title 'That the Crown of Scotland was not subject to England'—a subject to which Mackenzie returned in two shorter books published in 1685 and 1686—and introduces the Declaration thus:

'To show how great aversion even that generation had, for any such submission to the English monarchy, I have set down the copy of a letter yet extant, under all the seals of our nobility, directed to Pope John, in *anno* 1320. Therein they declare, that if their King should offer to submit to England, they would disown him, and chuse another. Not that the power of electing kings, was ever thought to reside in our nobility; but because it was represented to them, as the opinion of all lawyers, that a king could not alienat his kingdom, or submit himself by his sole consent, to a forreigne prince: since by that alienation and submission, he does forfeit his right to the crown.'

Mackenzie's next two pages are filled by a complete though not quite perfect Latin text of the Letter. There is no translation.[8] Mackenzie says nothing of the location of the document he is copying, but from his phrase 'yet extant, under all the seals of our nobility' there is no doubt that he saw and transcribed our document and that it then still bore all or most of the forty-six seals originally attached to it.

It was certainly at Tyninghame when transcribed by Gilbert Burnet, afterwards Bishop of Salisbury, who printed the text in 1683, including it rather incongruously in an appendix of miscellaneous documents added to the second volume of his *History of the Reformation of the Church of England*; for in a marginal note he says, '*Ex Autogr. apud Ill. Com. de H [addington.]*'[9] He probably saw and copied the document many years before 1683, during the four and a half years, from 1664 to 1669, when he was Episcopal minister of

39

East Saltoun and had a house not far from Tyninghame, just outside Haddington, which stood till twenty years ago.

Burnet may well have been the first person to transcribe the document at Tyninghame but Mackenzie certainly did not copy Burnet's transcription. They took independent views of some doubtful words: on the other hand, one seems to have copied some interpretations from the other. Both, I am sure, had seen the document. At a place in line 26 where a little of the text had perished along a fold in the parchment Burnet left a blank, noting in the margin, '*Quaedam sunt deleta*', but Mackenzie conjecturally filled in three words. The *Scotichronicon* text shows that Mackenzie guessed wrong, and also shows that neither he nor Burnet knew of its existence.

The next appearance of the Latin text was in a pamphlet of four leaves printed in Edinburgh in 1689 and accompanied for the first time by a translation into English. The Latin text is acknowledged to be taken from Sir George Mackenzie's book. There is nothing to tell who was the author of the English text, but it is an excellent translation, clear, and dignified, if at times a little free.

There was, I think, a topical reason for reprinting the Declaration of Arbroath at this time. To a generation taught, as men of the thirteenth century were not, that kings reigned by divine right, the most novel and startling passage in it was the affirmation that a king might be driven from his kingdom by his subjects 'as our enemy and a subverter of his own rights and ours', which Mackenzie, as we have seen, interpreted as meaning that 'a king could not alienat his kingdom . . . since by that alienation . . . he does forfeit his right to the crown'. King James VII had certainly not alienated either of his kingdoms, and Sir George Mackenzie, loyal to him as he had been to Charles II, voted in a minority of five against Sir John Dalrymple's revolutionary motion in the Parliament of Scotland on 4 April 1689.[10] That motion, carried by an overwhelming majority, declared that the King had 'invaded the fundamentall constitution of this kingdom and altered it from a legal limited monarchie to ane arbitrary despotick power . . . inverting all the ends of government, whereby he hath forefaulted the right to the croune and the throne is become vacant'. A week later the Estates resolved to offer the crown of Scotland to the King and Queen of England, William and Mary of Orange.[11] It might be argued that this was the one occasion on which the people of Scotland adopted a resolution from the Declaration of Arbroath and put it into action, considering their King as their enemy and a subverter of his own rights and theirs. Hence the ancient Letter of 1320 could have been read with a new and stern approval as the pamphlet circulated in Edinburgh at this time.

But the pamphlet was reprinted in 1702, again in both Latin and English, and with a different topical application. Now there was talk of Union with England, but also much resentment against recent English behaviour. In the autumn of that year the Parliament of Scotland was even considering altering the succession to the crown of Scotland after Queen Anne's death if Scottish demands regarding overseas trade were not satisfied. Interest in the Arbroath Declaration now centred not on the clauses threatening the ejection of an erring sovereign but on those asserting a nation's right to its freedom, 'which no honest man will give up but with life itself'; and now those famous phrases were printed in significant italics.

A considerable Anglo-Scottish pamphlet war raged during the years just before the Union of 1707; and one pamphlet on the English side revived the old claims of Edward I and Henry VIII that the kings of England had suzerainty over Scotland. It was written by William Atwood, an elderly, well-read, and extremely quarrelsome English barrister, and appeared in 1704.[12] In 1705 the Scottish Parliament declared it scurrilous and had it burnt by the common hangman,[13] and it was answered by James Anderson, Writer to the Signet, a man of much greater learning, who had for many years been working towards publishing a collection of major Scottish historical documents, for which design the Scottish Parliament in its very last weeks of existence voted him two grants of money.[14] Anderson refuted what he called 'the unbecoming artifices' of Atwood in a book entitled *An Historical Essay, shewing that the Crown of Scotland is Imperial and Independent* and in it printed a fresh transcription of the 1320 Declaration and another translation of it. He introduced them thus:

'The next monument of our independency in those days, is the known letter by the nobility and community to the Pope in the year 1320. It has been published both in Scotland and England'— he is referring evidently to Mackenzie's and Burnet's books—'but some words being wanting, and others mistaken, I have by the courtesie of the noble person in whose hands there is a fair original, with most of the seals intire, given a more exact copy of it in the appendix'.

His appendix no. 11 is accordingly the Latin text and no. 13 an English translation. In each case he departs from the strict objectivity of an editor to print the warning to King Robert in special type, capitals in the Latin text and italics in the English, and LIBERTATEM in the one and LIBERTY in the other are similarly given emphatic capitals.[15]

Anderson's translation was extensively quoted by Dr Patrick Abercromby in his book published in 1711, *The Martial Atchievements of the Scots Nation*, a favourite work of Sir Walter Scott's.[16]

In 1716 and 1722 appeared the two volumes of the collected works of Sir George Mackenzie, who had died in 1691. His *Observations upon Precedency* were reprinted in the second volume, but the third chapter, translated into Latin, had appeared as a separate essay in the first volume. There are thus two other versions of Mackenzie's 1680 text of the Arbroath Declaration, of which the 1722 one is the more accurate. George Crawfurd also printed a text based on Mackenzie's in 1726.[17]

Anderson's text, without a translation, was reprinted in 1739 in his great collection of engraved facsimiles of historical documents known to every historian of Scotland as 'Anderson's *Diplomata*'[18] Anderson, disappointed and unappreciated, had died eleven years before and his book appeared under the editorship of Thomas Ruddiman. The pamphlet of 1689 was reprinted in the *Harleian Miscellany* of 1744—and again at Glasgow in the third volume of the *Miscellanea Scotica* in 1820.

To all these reprints the first publication of the *Scotichronicon* in 1759, edited by Walter Goodall in two handsome folio volumes, added a slightly improved text. Thus before the death of George II the Declaration had been printed, in one form or another, eleven times in Latin and four times in English, and far from being neglected was well known, mainly perhaps through Anderson's *Diplomata*. The young James Boswell was familiar with it, probably from a copy of the *Diplomata* in his father's great library at Auchinleck, and when he noticed another copy of that work in a library in Leipzig took it down and read 'some choice passages' from the Declaration of Arbroath to his companions, a Dutch baron and a German professor, who, he recorded, 'were struck with the noble sentiments of liberty of the old Scots'.[19] Four years later he used the famous sentence preferring freedom to glory, riches or honours as a motto for the title-page of his *Account of Corsica*.

The Declaration had considerable notice from Lord Hailes, who gave nearly three pages of his *Annals of Scotland* to a rather free translation of most of it, citing Anderson and the *Scotichronicon* as his sources, and adding some valuable notes.[20]

Facsimile of the Register House copy of the Declaration, from the engraving in Anderson's Diplomata (1739).

Litera Comitum Baronum, Libere-

Sanctissimo Patri in xpo ac dno dno Johanni diuina prouidencia Sacrosancte R[omane]
Ranulphi Comes moravie dns mannie et vallis anandie. Patricius de Dumbar, C[omes]
Magnus Comes Cathanie et Orcadie et Willmus Comes Sutherlandie. Walterus Sen[escallus]
dns de Brechyn. Dauid de Graham. Ingram de Vmfrauill. Johannes de Menetet[h]
Scocie. Henr de sco Claro. Johes de Graham. Dauid de Lindesay. Willmus Olifaunt. [...]
[...] de Ardrossane Eustachius de Maxwell. Willms de Ramesay Willms de Monte ab[...]
de Lescelyn & Alex de Stratoun ceteriq; Barones et Liberetenentes ac tota Communitas Re[gni]
et ex antiquorum gestis et libris collegimus q; inter ceteras naciones egregias nostra Scilicet Sco[torum]
ens et in hispania nec ferocissimos p multa tempum cumulacula Residens? a nullis quant[um]cumque
tia sibi sedes in occidente quas nunc optinet expulsis Britonibus, & Pictis omnino de[letis]
adquisiuit ipasq; ab omni seruitute liberas vt Priscorum testant historie semp tenuit.
Nobilitates & merita licet ex aliis non clarerent satis patere effulgent ex eo q Rex Re[gum]
dem sanctissimum conuocauit si eos p quemlibet in dca fide confirmari voluit sz p sm[...] p[...]
Patronum Hec ante sanctissimi Patres & Predecessores vri sollicita mente pensantes ip[...]
ipsorum precione libera hacten degunt & quieta doi ille princeps magnificus Rex Anglorum E[...]
tute assumi ob annua & confederati specie inumabilit infestauit Cui iniurias cedes & v[...]
alia quoq; enormia que in dco poplo exercuit ulli pciens etati aut sexui Religioni aut ordi[...]
milia medetur & sanat libertati siui p Strenuissimum Principem Regem & dnm nrm dnm [...]
medias & picta leto sustinuit animo. qui etiam Diuina disposicio, & iuxta leges & Consuet[udines]
rite principe atq; Regem Cui tang illi p qui salus in poplo facta est, pro nra libertate tue[nda]
nos aut Regnum ipm volens subiici tang Inimicum nrm & suu nrum q; Iuris subuersorem statu[...]
rint integ Anglorum dno aliquem volumus subiugari Non em ppt gliam, Diuicias aut honores pu[gnamus]
omni penam iustancia genuflexis cordibus exorauit gm Sincero corde mente pia recensentes q a[...]
angustias nobis & Ecclie dei illatas ab Anglicis, pacuis oculis intuentes? Regem Anglorum cui s[...]
vt nos scotos in exili degentes scocia vlt q'in habitacio non est mchilq; u nrm Cupiente
effectu. vest em nidest sce Pat hoc facere qui paganorum feritatem chanorum culpis exigen[...]
Ecclia in aliqua sui pte nris tempibz paciat eclipsim aut Scandalum vos videntis. Ex
quas hui cui penuis ire no posse Cui impedimenti Causa est Veror (q in moribus penuis
Anglorum nos in pace diuidere illic venir qui mchil ignorat satis nouit Et nos, si vicario[...]
bet aut ipis in nram confusionem fauere no desinat corpus exardia atamq; exardia & cetia qu[...]
in his que tenem tang obediencie filij vob tang ipius vicario in omnibz coplacere ipidq; q[...]
qui nob vtentem facere tand mchil in redigat hostes nros. Statem ac sanitatem vram c[...]
Aprilis. Anno gre Millesimo Trescentesimo Vicesimo. Anno v Regni Regis nri Supra[...]

...clesie Summo Pontifici. filij sui humiles et deuoti Dunecanus Comes de ffyff Thomas
... Comes de Stratherne Malcolmus Comes de Leuenax Willms Comes de Ross
... de Soules Buttelar Scocie Jacobus Dus de Duglas. Rogus de Moubray. Dauid
... meneteth. Alexr frae. Gilbtus de Haya Constabular Scoc. Robtus de keth marescallus
... annes de ffenton. Willms de Abirnithi. Dauid de Wemys. Willms de Monte fixo. ffergu
... Donenaldus Cambell. Johannes Cambrun Regnaldus le chen. Alex de Seton. Andreas

... reuerentiam filialem cu deuotis pedum osculis beator. Scim sanctissime pat vie,
... huius fuerunt insignita que de q̃ maiori scibtha p mare treum et Columpnas herculis trus
... at alicubi subiugari. Judeos veniens post mille et Ducentos annos a xpisti ppli israeli
... tenses Datos et Anglicos sepius inpugnata fuere diutus sibi victorijs et labozibz q̃ plurimis
... et Tresdecim Reges de ipor Regali psapia nullo alienigena inteueniente Regnauerint. Quor
... passionem et Resurreccionem suam ipos in ultimis tre finibz constitutos quasi pmos ad suam fi
... scdm uel tciu sancti Andree q̃ mitissimu beatu pet germanu que semp ipos pesse uoluit ut
... beati pet p ginam peculiar Diutis fauoribz et puilegijs q̃ plurimis q̃ nunc tueri. Ita q̃ gens m̃a sub
... iunc est Regnu n̄rm acephalu ppulu q̃ ullius mali aut doli conscium n bellis aut insultibz
... cendia plator mercacones monasthior cobustiones Religiosor spliacones et occisiones
... in plenum intelligeret n qui experiencia informaret A quibz malis innumeris ipo Jnuante q̃ post
... hereditate suis de manibz Jnimicor libandis gti alt machabeus aut Josue labozi et cedia
... ad mortem suftinere uolumt Juris successio et Debit ipor omn Consensus et assensus n̄rm fece
... ... et uolum in omnibz adherere. Cui si ab inceptis desifteret Regi Anglor aut Anglicis
... in Regem n̄rm qui ad defensionem n̄ram sufficeret faciend. Cu m̃a q̃ dum certu cu̅ remanse
... solummodo qui Nemo bon̄ n sumul aduita amitit. Hinc est Reuende pat et Dne q̃ sacratem u̅iam
... ... gentis n̄os sic Pondus et pondus n distinctio Judei et greci scoti aut Anglici tribulacones et
... Dei cu olim Anglia septemart ptibz solebat sufficere Regibz monere et exhortari dignemini
... ... p uia procuranda quiete quicquid possum ad statu n̄rm Respectu hico fade uolum ut
... ... aspicitis et xanor Dinos arctari in Dies q ...... acis memorie Deuoti si q̃ d absq̃
... apes qui uo causam uel causam pu̅entes se fingunt in subsidiu tre scē xpisti sueuras
... pior et resistencia Debilior est inuar. Set q̃ uero corde dictus Dns Rex n̄r et Nos si Rex
... ... et testamn quibz si scitas uia Anglor relatibz nimis credula fidem sinceram non adhi
... ... ipi in nob et Nos in ipis fecim cob ab altissimo credimu inpitanda ex quo s̄m̄ tenui
... causam n̄ram tuendam commitim Cogitatu n̄rm Jactantes in ipo spantes q̃ fuit
... ... sue scē p tempa Diutina. Dat apud Monasthiu de Abir-brothoc in Scocia sexto die
... ... no - --

The original copper plate still survives for the magnificent engraving of the Tyninghame document which James Anderson caused to be made for his *Diplomata*. The engraver is said to have been 'Basire'.[21] This must have been Isaac Basire, the father of the better-known James Basire, and he must have executed the plate when he was still young and Anderson was near the end of his life, for Isaac Basire was born only in 1704. The engraving is a meticulously careful copy of every pen-stroke in the original manuscript; but it stops at the end of the text with no reproduction of the folded foot of the parchment nor of the tags and seals it then bore, though it appears that thirty-nine of the original forty-six still survived at that time. We owe Anderson and Basire a great debt for this engraving, since it preserves the entire text except for the two words in the damaged line that had bothered Mackenzie and Burnet. At some time during the eighteenth century the document suffered serious damage through damp, so that today it shows two large ragged gaps in which considerable portions of the text have vanished.

In 1812, when Thomas Thomson, Deputy Clerk Register, was preparing the text for the publication of the Acts of the Parliament of Scotland, the 8th Earl of Haddington gave permission for the copying of the seals attached to the Declaration of Arbroath, twenty-one of which still remained of the original forty-six, though today there are only nineteen.[22] The opportunity was taken to make a complete reproduction of the whole document. Because of the gaps, Basire's plate was used, a new engraving made of the lower portion with the tags and surviving seals, and the two blended against a coloured background to represent the old parchment. This combination of engravings may have been completed before September 1815,[23] but was not finally published till 1844. It bears the name 'W. & D. Lizars', indicating the well-known artist and engraver William Lizars whose father Daniel died in 1812. This plate is also still preserved. It was used again in the *National Manuscripts of Scotland* in 1870, and also for an edition of engraving, text, and translation taken from that work and distributed by the Burns Federation to Scottish schools a few years ago.

In August 1829 the 9th Earl of Haddington, 'in pursuance of the directions of his father, the late Earl',[24] restored the precious document to the Register House, since which time it has been on permanent exhibition mounted in a specially made frame. In 1967 its condition was carefully examined and the seals cleaned, and for the first time it was photographed.

43

There have been two fresh publications of the text in recent years. One, with a new and excellent English translation, was given by the late R. L. Mackie in the *Scots Magazine* in 1934. The other, the first attempt at a collated text, using Thomson's, Mackenzie's of 1716, and Goodall's *Scotichronicon*, was printed by the late Lord President Cooper in his stimulating little book *Supra Crepidam* in 1951, and was also accompanied by a translation.[25] Of modern translations besides these two, Professor R. K. Hannay's must be mentioned, done from Goodall's text collated with Thomson's. This, with a few changes and one or two phrases borrowed from Lord Cooper's version, was used in the recent collection *A Source Book of Scottish History*.[26]

Following up the belated discovery in 1944 that the often-quoted phrase about 'neither glory, nor riches, nor honours' was an adapted passage from Sallust,[27] Lord Cooper analysed the whole text of the Declaration, finding it 'replete with apt quotations' and, as he put it, 'practically set to music' by its skilful use of the *ars dictaminis*. It is evident that the early Victorian schoolmaster 'who used this Letter as an exercise for his boys in Latin, holding that its patriotism covered any defects of Latinity',[28] needed no apology, but it was left to Lord Cooper to perceive and point out its literary merits. He did this from the study of three printed texts. In my own version which follows I have tried to answer the plea of that eminent judge, great scholar, and historian *manqué*, for 'a scientifically collated text founded on these sources and any others which may exist'.[29]

NOTES

[1] *Exchequer Rolls*, i, pp. lxxv, 114.

[2] *Treasurer's Accounts*, vii, p. 337.

[3] W. A. Craigie: *The Maitland Quarto Manuscript*, Scottish Text Society, New Series 9, p. 66b. I have modified the spelling.

[4] But Professor Trever-Roper attributes to Buchanan a memorandum presented by the Earl of Morton to Queen Elizabeth's commissioners in 1571, which contains the words: 'wherein the nobilitie and people of Scotland, defending their aunctient and laudable custome and their lawe, rather spent their blode than they wold suffer their libertie fall and decaye' (H. R. Trevor-Roper, 'George Buchanan and the Ancient Scottish Constitution', *English Historical Review*, Supplement 3, p. 47).

[5] Quoted in *A.P.S.*, i, p. 28.

[6] *The Historical Works of Sir James Balfour*, 1825, i, pp. 98–100.

[7] *Accounts of the Master of Works*, i, pp. 325, 326, 328; Robertson's *Index,,* 1798, p. xlvi; *Tenth Annual Report of the Deputy Clerk Register*, pp. 9–10.

[8] *Observations upon the Laws and Customs of Nations as to Precedency, by Sir George Mackenzie of Rosehaugh, His Majesty's Advocate in the Kingdom of Scotland*, 1680, pp. 19–21.

[9] *The History of the Reformation of the Church of England, The Second Part, by Gilbert Burnet, D.D.*, 1683: (Appendix) *A Collection of Records and Original Papers*, pp. 109–11.

[10] G. W. T. Omond: *The Lord Advocates of Scotland*, i, p. 232.

[11] *A.P.S.*, ix, pp. 34, 40.

[12] William Atwood: *The Superiority and Direct Dominion of the Imperial Crown of England over the Crown and Kingdom of Scotland*, London, 1704. On Atwood's life and character see *D.N.B.*

[13] *A.P.S.*, ix, p. 221.   [14] *Ibid.*, pp. 427–8.

[15] James Anderson: *An Historical Essay*, &c., Edinburgh, 1705.

[16] Vol. i, pp. 610–11.

[17] *The Works of that Eminent and Learned Lawyer Sir George Mackenzie of Rosehaugh*, vol. i, (Edinburgh, 1716): *Treatises*, pp. 145–6; ii (1722), pp. 526–8; *Lives . . . of the Officers . . . of the State*, pp. 432–4.

[18] *Selectus Diplomatum et Numismatum Scotiae Thesaurus*, 1739, nos. LI, LII.

[19] *Boswell on the Grand Tour: Germany and Switzerland*, ed. Pottle, 1953, pp. 125–6.

[20] *Annals of Scotland*, 1776, ii, pp. 93–5. In Hailes's first edition the reference to the *Scotichronicon* is confused by the misprinting of 'Fordun as 'Foedera'.

[21] *National Manuscripts of Scotland*, ii, p. viii.

[22] *Fifth Annual Report of the Deputy Clerk Register*, App. p. 34.

[23] *Ninth Annual Report*, p. 11.   [24] *A.P.S.*, i, p. 291.

[25] *Scots Magazine*, new series, xxi, no. 1, pp. 9–18; *Supra Crepidam*, 1951, pp. 62–71.

[26] R. K. Hannay: *The Letter of the Barons of Scotland to Pope John XXII in 1320*, 1936; Dickinson, Donaldson and Milne: *A Source Book of Scottish History*, i (1952), pp. 131–5.

[27] *Scottish Historical Review*, xxvi, p. 75.

[28] *National Manuscripts of Scotland*, loc. cit.

[29] *Supra Crepidam*, p. 49.

3

LETTER OF THE BARONS

OF SCOTLAND TO THE POPE

6 APRIL M CCC XX.

ORIGINAL TEXT RECONSTRUCTED

from the draft preserved in Scotichronicon
and the contemporary copy (imperfect)
in HM General Register House

NOTE

In framing my attempt at a definitive text I have noted not only the variants between manuscripts but many of the amendments, conjectures and in some cases vagaries and errors of successive editors. Contemplating the work of these many eminent men and great scholars, I cannot hope to have escaped all errors myself, but like them I have done my best.

I follow in general the spelling of the only extant contemporary manuscript—the defective file copy now in the Register House which I have called Tyn—and ignore in my variorum notes such alternatives as *Scocia* and *Scotia, vestre* and *vestrae, sed* and *set, occulis* and *oculis, quatenus* and *quatinus, inputanda* and *imputanda*. Among the wide variations in spelling proper names I have noted only the few that seem of interest.

I have carefully retained the capital initials used by the scribe of Tyn. Apart from those often given to principal nouns and verbs, they seem sometimes to be used for deliberate emphasis: *Centum et Tresdecim Reges* (11), *Consensus et Assensus* (19), *Centum ex nobis* (21), *Nemo bonus* (22), *Nos in ipsis fecerimus* (30), as well as with an almost ironical punctilio for *ille Princeps Magnificus Rex Anglorum Edwardus* (15). I have, however, followed my own judgment in punctuation and paragraphing. The original is, of course, unparagraphed.

REFERENCES TO COLLATED TEXTS

Tyn = MS copy formerly at Tyninghame, now in HM General Register House, SRO SP 13/7, 1320.

Sc = *Scotichronicon* MSS generally; ScE, MS Edinburgh University Library, MS 186; ScC, MS Corpus Christi College, Cambridge, 171; ScR, MS British Museum, Royal Library, 13 EX; ScB, MS formerly at Brechin Castle, now in HM General Register House, SRO GD 45/26/48; ScL, MS National Library of Scotland, Adv. 35.1.7.
All these MSS are described by W. F. Skene in *The Historians of Scotland*, vol. I, pp. xv-xviii.

Prints

B = Gilbert Burnet: *History of the Reformation*, 1683.

R = Sir George Mackenzie of Rosehaugh generally; R1, *Observations on Precedency*, 1680; R2, *Causae Forenses* in *Works*, vol. i, 1716; Rc, *Observations* repr. in *Works*, vol. ii, 1722.

A = James Anderson generally; A1, *Historical Essay*, 1705; A2, *Diplomata*: transcript from facsimile, 1739.

G = Walter Goodall in his edition of *Scotichronicon*, 1759.

T = Thomas Thomson in *Acts of the Parliament of Scotland*, 1844.

N = Cosmo Innes in *National Manuscripts of Scotland*, 1870.

M = R. L. Mackie in *Scots Magazine*, April 1934.

C = Lord Cooper in *Supra Crepidam*, 1951.

ORIGINAL TEXT RECONSTRUCTED

1 SANCTISSIMO PATRI IN CHRISTO AC DOMINO,
domino Johanni, diuina prouidencia Sacrosancte[1]
Romane et Vniuersalis Ecclesie Summo Pontifici, Filii
Sui Humiles et deuoti Duncanus Comes de Fyf, Thomas
2 Ranulphi Comes Morauie Dominus Mannie et Vallis
Anandie, Patricius de Dumbar Comes Marchie, Malisius
Comes de Stratheryne, Malcolmus Comes de Leuenax,
Willelmus Comes de Ross,
3 Magnus Comes Cathanie et Orkadie et Willelmus Comes
Suthirlandie; Walterus Senescallus Scocie, Willelmus
de Soules Buttelarius Scocie,[2] Jacobus Dominus[3] de
Duglas, Rogerus de Moubray,[4] Dauid
4 Dominus[3] de Brechyn, Dauid de Graham, Ingeramus de
Vmfrauille, Johannes de Menetethe Custos Comitatus
de Menetethe,[5] Alexander Fraser, Gilbertus de Haya
Constabularius
5 Scocie, Robertus de Keth Marescallus Scocie, Henricus[6]
de Sancto Claro,[7] Johannes de Graham, Dauid de
Lindesay, Willelmus Olifaunt,[8] Patricius de Graham,
Johannes de Fentoun, Willelmus de Abirnithy, Dauid de
Wemys, Willelmus de Montefixo, Fergu-
6 sius de Ardrossane, Eustachius de Maxwell, Willelmus
de Ramesay, Willelmus de Montealto,[9] Alanus de
Morauia, Douenaldus Cambell, Johannes Cambrun,[10]
Reginaldus le chen, Alexander de Setoun, Andreas
7 de Lescelyne,[11] et Alexander de Stratoun, Ceterique
Barones et Liberetenentes ac tota Communitas Regni
Scocie, omnimodam Reuerenciam filialem cum deuotis
Pedum osculis beatorum.

[1] Tyn, T, N, M *Sacrosauncte;* C *sacrosante.*
[2] ScB places this name after *Dauid de Graham* infra.
[3] Sc omits.   [4] Sc omits this name.
[5] Sc *custos comitatus eiusdem.*   [6] ScB *Willelmus.*
[7] Sc, G *Sancto Claro panetarius Scocie.*   [8] Sc omits this name.
[9] Sc omits this name.   [10] Sc *Cameron.*
[11] Sc *Lesly*

Scimus, Sanctissime Pater et Domine,

8   et ex antiquorum gestis et libris Colligimus quod inter
Ceteras naciones egregias nostra scilicet Scottorum
nacio multis preconijs fuerit insignita, que de Maiori
Schithia[12] per Mare tirenum[13] et Columpnas[14]
Herculis transi-

9   ens et in Hispania inter ferocissimas gentes[15] per multa
temporum curricula Residens a nullis[16] quantumcumque[17] barbaricis poterat allicubi gentibus[18]
subiugari. Indeque veniens post mille et[19] ducentos
annos a transitu populi israeli-

10 tici per mare rubrum[20] sibi sedes in Occidente quas
nunc optinet,[21] expulsis primo[22] Britonibus et Pictis
omnino deletis, licet per Norwagienses, Dacos[23] et
Anglicos[24] sepius inpugnata fuerit,[25] multis cum[26]
victorijs et Laboribus quamplurimis

11 adquisiuit, ipsasque ab omni seruitute liberas, vt
Priscorum[27] testantur Historie, semper tenuit. In quorum
Regno Centum et Tresdecim[28] Reges de ipsorum
Regali prosapia, nullo alienigena interueniente,
Regnauerunt.

Quorum[29]

12 Nobilitates[30] et Merita, licet ex aliis
non clarerent, satis[31] patenter[32] effulgent ex eo quod
Rex Regum et[33] dominancium[34] dominus[35] Jhesus Christus post passionem suam et Resurreccionem[36] ipsos in
vltimis terre finibus[37] constitutos quasi primos[38] ad suam fi-

13 dem sanctissimam conuocauit.[39] Nec eos per quemlibet
in dicta fide confirmari voluit set per suum primum

[12] Sc *de Grecie finibus et Egipti.*
[13] B, G, *Tyrrhenum.*   [14] ScL *calumpnas*; B, R, G, C *columnas.*
[15] Tyn and all editors omit *gentes* and read *ferocissimos.*
[16] ScC, ScR *nonnullis.*   [17] ScL *quantumque.*   [18] Tyn and all editors omit.
[19] Sc omits.   [20] Tyn and all editors omit these three words.
[21] ScE, ScC, ScR, ScB *optet*; B, R, G, C *obtinet.*
[22] Tyn and all editors omit.   [23] R followed by C *Danos.*   [24] R, C *Anglos.*
[25] Sc *fuerat.*   [26] Tyn and all editors *sibi.*   [27] Sc *prisce.*
[28] ScE, ScC *tredecim*; ScB, R2 *tredecem*; ScL, B, R1, R3 *tresdecem.*
[29] ScL *Horum*, beginning a new chapter with a coloured initial.
[30] ScB *libertates.*   [31] R, C *satis tamen.*   [32] ScB *potenter.*
[33] B, R omit.   [34] Tyn and all editors omit.   [35] Sc *dominus noster.*
[36] Tyn and all editors *passionem et Resurreccionem suam.*
[37] Sc *finibus terre.*   [38] ScB *primo.*   [39] ScL *conuocauit sanctissimam.*

apostolum vocacione[40] quamuis ordine secundum vel
tercium, sanctum[41] Andream mitissimum[42] beati Petri
Germanum, quem semper ipsis preesse voluit vt
14 Patronum.[43]
     Hec autem Sanctissimi Patres et
Predecessores vestri sollicita mente pensantes ipsum
Regnum et[44] populum vt beati Petri germani peculium
multis fauoribus et priuilegijs quamplurimis Munierunt,[45]
Ita quippe quod[46] gens nostra sub
15 ipsorum proteccione hactenus libera[47] deguit[48] et quieta
donec ille Princeps Magnificus Rex Anglorum Edwardus,[49]
pater istius qui nunc est, Regnum nostrum acephalum
populumque nullius mali aut doli conscium[50] nec bellis aut
insultibus
16 tunc assuetum sub amici et confederati[51] specie inimicabiliter[52] infestauit. Cuius iniurias, Cedes,[53] violencias, predaciones, incendia, prelatorum incarceraciones, Monasteriorum combustiones, Religiosorum spoliaciones et occisiones
17 alia quoque enormia et innumera[54] que in dicto populo
exercuit,[55] nulli parcens etati aut sexui, Religioni aut ordini,
nullus scriberet nec ad plenum intelligeret nisi quem experiencia informaret.
     A quibus Malis innumeris, ipso Juuante qui post uulnera
18 medetur et sanat, liberati sumus per strenuissimum[56] Principem, Regem et Dominum nostrum,[57] Dominum[58] Robertum, qui pro populo et hereditate suis de manibus Inimicorum

[40] Tyn and all editors but G and C omit.
[41] Tyn and all editors but B and R *scilicet.*
[42] B, R *meritissimum.*
[43] With the next sentence ScE, ScC, ScR, ScB begin, with a coloured
initial, a new chapter; followed by G.
[44] ScC *ut.*   [45] B *muniverunt.*
[46] Tyn, G, T, N, M *Ita quod*; B, R, A, C *Itaque.*
[47] Tyn and all editors *libera hactenus.*
[48] ScL (*decuit* deleted) *deguit*; B *degit.*
[49] Sc *Eadwardus Rex Anglie.*
[50] ScE, ScC, ScR, ScB *mali doli conscium*; ScL *mali conscium doli.*
[51] B *amica et confederata.*   [52] B, R *innumerabiliter.*
[53] Tyn, ScB and all editors *Cedes et.*
[54] ScB *innormia et innumera*; Tyn and all editors omit *et innumera.*
[55] Tyn, T, N, M *excercuit.*   [56] B, R *serenissimum.*
[57] ScR omits *Regem*; ScB omits *nostrum*; ScL *principem et dominum
nostrum regem.*
[58] ScL, A omit; ScB *dominum nostrum*; B, G *D.*

liberandis quasi[59] alter Machabeus aut Josue labores et tedia,

19 inedias et pericula, leto sustinuit animo. Quem eciam diuina disposicio et[60] iuxta leges et Consuetudines nostra, quas vsque ad[61] mortem sustinere volumus, Juris successio et debitus nostrorum omnium[62] Consensus et Assensus nostrum fece-

20 runt Principem atque[63] Regem, cui tanquam illi per quem salus in populo nostro[64] facta est pro nostra libertate tuenda tam Jure quam meritis tenemur et volumus in omnibus adherere.

Quem si ab inceptis
desisteret,[65] regi[66] Anglorum aut Anglicis

21 nos[67] aut Regnum[68] nostrum volens subicere,[69] tanquam inimicum nostrum et sui nostrique Juris subuersorem statim expellere niteremur[70] et alium Regem nostrum qui ad defensionem nostram sufficeret faceremus.[71] Quia quamdiu Centum ex nobis[72] viui[73]

22 remanserint, nuncquam Anglorum dominio aliquatenus volumus[74] subiugari. Non[75] enim propter gloriam,[76] diuicias aut honores pugnamus set propter libertatem[77] solummodo quam Nemo bonus nisi simul cum vita amittit.[78]

Hinc est, Reuerende [79] Pater et Domine,
quod sanctitatem vestram

23 omni[80] precum instancia genuflexis cordibus[81] exoramus quatinus sincero corde Menteque[82] pia recensentes quod[83] apud eum cuius vices in terris[84] geritis cum[85] non sit Pondus[86] nec distinccio Judei et greci, Scoti aut[87] Anglici, tribulaciones et

24 angustias nobis et Ecclesie dei illatas ab Anglicis paternis occulis intuentes, Regem[88] Anglorum, cui sufficere debet

---

[59] ScE, ScC, ScB, ScL *velut* ; ScR *velud.*   [60] ScL omits.   [61] ScR omits.
[62] R omits.   [63] B *ac.*   [64] Tyn and all editors omit.   [65] B, R *desistet.*
[66] G *et regi.*   [67] ScB omits.   [68] ScR *regem.*   [69] B, R, A, G, C *subjicere.*
[70] B, R3 *nitemur.*   [71] B, R *sufficiet faciemus.*
[72] Tyn and all editors omit these two words.   [73] C *viri.*
[74] ScE, ScC, ScR, ScL *volumus aliquatenus* ; ScB ends a column with *dominio*, omits *aliquatenus* and begins a new page with *Volumus.*
[75] ScL here begins a new column with a coloured initial.
[76] Sc *gloriam belli.*   [77] Sc *leges paternas et libertatem.*   [78] B, R2 *amittet.*
[79] Sc *Sanctissime.*   [80] R *cum omni.*   [81] Sc omits these two words.
[82] ScB *mente.*   [83] ScR *et.*   [84] ScB *terra.*   [85] Tyn and all editors omit.
[86] Tyn and all editors *Pondus et pondus.*   [87] Sc *vel.*
[88] ScC, ScR, ScL *regi* ; ScE, ScB *regis.*

quod possidet cum olim Anglia septem aut pluribus solebat
sufficere Regibus, Monere et[89] exhortari[90] dignemini
25 vt nos scotos, in exili degentes Scocia vltra quam habitacio
non est nichilque nisi nostrum Cupientes, in pace dimittat.[91]
Cui pro nostra procuranda quiete quicquid possumus, ad
statum nostrum[92] Respectu habito, facere[93] volumus cum
26 effectu.[94]
  Vestra enim interest,[95] sancte Pater, hoc
facere qui paganorum feritatem, Christianorum culpis exigentibus, in Christianos seuientem aspicitis et Christianorum
terminos arctari indies,[96] quantumque vestre[97] sanctitatis[98]
memorie[99] derogat[100] si (quod absit)
27 Ecclesia in aliqua sui parte vestris temporibus patiatur[101]
eclipsim[102] aut Scandalum,[103] vos videritis. Excitet[104] igitur
Christianos[105] Principes qui non causam vt causam ponentes
se fingunt in subsidium terre sancte propter guerras
28 quas habent cum proximis ire non posse.[106] Cuius inpedimenti[107] Causa est verior[108] quod in Minoribus proximis
debellandis vtilitas propior et resistencia debilior estimantur.[109] Set quam leto corde dictus dominus Rex noster[110]
et Nos si Rex
29 Anglorum nos in pace dimitteret[111] illuc iremus qui nichil
ignorat[112] satis novit. Quod Christi vicario[113] totique
Christianitati ostendimus et testamur.
  Quibus si sanctitas vestra Anglorum
relatibus nimis credula fidem sinceram non[114]
30 adhibeat[115] aut ipsis in nostram confusionem fauere non
desinat, corporum excidia, animarum[116] exicia,[117] et cetera

---

[89] ScE omits.   [90] ScR *exortari*.   [91] R1 *dimittet*.
[92] ScR, ScB, ScL *vestrum*.   [93] R, C *hoc facere*.   [94] ScB, T, M *affectu*.
[95] Sc *refert*.   [96] Tyn, T, N, M *artari in dies*.
[97] A's conjecture to fill a lacuna in Tyn, followed by G, N, M, C;
Sc *quantumcumque vestre*; R *quare ne quid vestre*; B, T *Q. . .*, B noting
'*Quaedam sunt deleta*'.   [98] C omits.   [99] ScL, G *memoria*.
[100] R1, R2, *derogat &*; R3 *deroget &*; C suggests *deroget*.
[101] ScL omits.   [102] ScB *ineclipsin*; B, R1, R3 *ecclipsin*; R2 *celipsin*.
[103] ScL *paciatur aut scandalum*.   [104] B, R1, R2 *Exhortet*.
[105] A2 *Chrianos*.   [106] ScR *possunt*.   [107] ScL *expedimenti*.
[108] ScL, R1, R3 *vereor*.   [109] Sc *estimatur*; G *aestimatur*.
[110] Sc *dominus noster rex predictus*.   [111] B *dimittit*; R *dimittet*; A2 *demitteret*.
[112] R1 *ignoret*.   [113] ScB *vocario*.   [114] Sc omits.
[115] Tyn, B, R1, R3, A, T, N, C *adhibet*; ScE *adhibebat*; M *adhibit*.
[116] T *animorum*.   [117] Sc *exterminia*.

que sequentur[118] incomoda que ipsi in nobis[119] et[120] Nos in ipsis fecerimus vobis[121] ab altissimo credimus inputanda.

Ex quo sumus et erimus

31 in hiis que tenemur[122] tanquam obediencie filii vobis tanquam ipsius vicario parati[123] in omnibus complacere, ipsique[124] tanquam Summo Regi et Judici causam nostram tuendam committimus, Cogitatum nostrum Jactantes[125] in ipso sperantesque[126] firmiter[127]

32 quod in nobis[128] virtutem faciet et ad nichilum rediget hostes nostros.

Sanctitatem[129] ac[130] sanitatem[131] vestram conseruet altissimus Ecclesie sue sancte per[132] tempora diuturna.

Datum apud Monasterium[133] de [134] Abirbrothoc[135] in Scocia Sexto die

33 mensis[136] Aprilis Anno gracie Millesimo Trescentesimo vicesimo[137] Anno[138] vero Regni[139] Regis nostri[140] supradicti[141] Quinto decimo.

Endorsed:[142] Littere directe ad dominum Supremum Pontificem per communitatem Scocie.

Names inscribed on some of the seal tags: Alexander de Lambertoun, Edwardus de Keth, Johannes de Inchmertyn, Thomas de Meiners, Johannes Duraunt, Thomas de Morham (and one illegible).

[118] ScE, ScC, ScB, ScL *secuntur*; ScR *sequntur.*   [119] ScB *in nobis ipsi.*
[120] ScC omits.   [121] ScC *vobis tanquam ipsius vicario pa* — struck through.
[122] C *tenemur parati.*
[123] Tyn and all editors omit but G and C who misplaces the word to follow *tenemur.*
[124] Sc *ipsi.*   [125] B *jactitantes.*   [126] Sc *sperantes.*   [127] B, R1, R2 *finem.*
[128] T, M *vobis.*   [129] B, R1, R2 *Serenitatem.*   [130] A2 *et.*
[131] B, R1, R2 *sanctitatem.*   [132] ScR *ad.*   [133] Sc *monasterium nostrum.*
[134] ScC, ScR, ScL omit.
[135] ScE, ScC, ScR, ScL *Abirbroth*; ScB *Abirbrotho*; B *Aberbroth*; R *Aberbrothock.*
[136] Tyn and all editors omit.   [137] ScE omits.
[138] ScE, ScR, ScB, ScL omit.
[139] ScE, ScC, ScB *regni vero*; ScR *regno*; ScL *regni quinto.*
[140] T omits.   [141] Sc *predicti.*
[142] Tyn, but all editors except B and M omit the endorsed words.

54